Home Office Research Study 222

Electronic monitoring of released prisoners: an evaluation of the Home Detention Curfew scheme

Kath Dodgson, Philippa Goodwin, Philip Howard, Siân Llewellyn-Thomas,
Ed Mortimer, Neil Russell and Mark Weiner

*"The views expressed in this report are those of the
authors, not necessarily those of the Home Office
(nor do they reflect Government policy)."*

Home Office Research, Development and Statistics Directorate
March 2001

Home Office Research Studies

The Home Office Research Studies are reports on research undertaken by or on behalf of the Home Office. They cover the range of subjects for which the Home Secretary has responsibility. Other publications produced by the Research, Development and Statistics Directorate include Research Findings, the Research Bulletin, Statistical Bulletins and Statistical Papers.

The Research, Development and Statistics Directorate

RDS is part of the Home Office. The Home Office's purpose is to build a safe, just and tolerant society in which the rights and responsibilities of individuals, families and communities are properly balanced and the protection and security of the public are maintained.

RDS is also a part of the Government Statistical Service (GSS). One of the GSS aims is to inform Parliament and the citizen about the state of the nation and provide a window on the work and performance of government, allowing the impact of government policies and actions to be assessed.

Therefore -

Research Development and Statistics Directorate exists to improve policy making, decision taking and practice in support of the Home Office purpose and aims, to provide the public and Parliament with information necessary for informed debate and to publish information for future use.

First published 2001
Application for reproduction should be made to the Communications and Development Unit, Room 201, Home Office, 50 Queen Anne's Gate, London SW1H 9AT.
© Crown copyright 2001   ISBN 1 84082 630 4
                           ISSN 0072 6435

Acknowledgements

We would like to thank all those who contributed to the preparation of this report, which was commissioned by colleagues in the Prisoner Administration Group and Sentence Enforcement Unit at Prison Service HQ and in the Electronic Monitoring Section of the Home Office.

We are grateful for the assistance given with collecting, analysing and interpreting the data by colleagues within the Research, Development and Statistics Directorate (RDS). Colleagues across RDS and other directorates in the Home Office and Prison Service also provided many useful comments on the content and structure of the report.

This evaluation contains findings from a survey of curfewees, family members and supervising probation officers, which was carried out by RSGB (part of the Taylor Nelson Sofres Group). We would particularly like to thank all those who agreed to be interviewed for this research. Thanks are also due to a number of other RSGB staff who contributed to the administration, interviewing, data entry, data quality and analysis for this survey.

Kath Dodgson
Philip Howard   Offenders and Corrections Unit, Home Office
Ed Mortimer

Philippa Goodwin
Siân Llewellyn-Thomas   RSGB
Neil Russell

Mark Weiner   Economics and Resource Analysis Unit, Home Office

March 2001

Contents

Summary

The Home Detention Curfew (HDC) scheme was introduced on 28 January 1999 across the whole of England and Wales. Most prisoners sentenced to at least three months but less than four years are eligible for release up to 60 days early on an electronically monitored curfew provided that they pass a risk assessment and have a suitable address.

This report draws together the main strands of an evaluation of the Home Detention Curfew scheme covering the first 16 months of the scheme. It includes: an analysis of release rates and recalls to prison; a survey of curfewees, family members and probation supervisors; a cost-benefit study of HDC; and an analysis of short-term reoffending by offenders released early onto the scheme compared to a control group.

The use of Home Detention Curfew

Prison and probation staff carry out an assessment of the suitability of an inmate for HDC and of the suitability of his/her proposed address. Of the 72,400 prisoners eligible for the scheme in the first 16 months, 30 per cent were granted early release on HDC following this risk assessment process (see Table 1).

Table 1:   HDC data for the first 16 months of operation

Numbers eligible to be considered for HDC	72,400
Numbers released on HDC	21,400
Release rate (as percentage of those eligible)	30%
Number recalled to prison	1,100
Recall rate (as percentage of those placed on HDC)	5%
Average number on curfew at any one time	2,000

N.B. All figures are rounded to the nearest 100.

Over the first 16 months of the scheme, over 21,000 inmates (an average of over 1,300 per month) were released on HDC to spend the last part of their custodial sentence on curfew in the community. At any one time, an average of just under 2,000 prisoners have been on HDC.

Of those released in this period, only five per cent were recalled to prison following a breakdown in their curfew. The main reasons for recall were breach of the curfew conditions (68% of recalls) or a change of circumstances (25%). Only eight curfewees (less than 1% of all recalls) were returned to custody because they represented a risk of serious harm to the public.

Variations in release and recall rates

Release rates vary considerably between different types of establishment and prisoner. Most of these differences appear to be related to risk of reconviction and reimprisonment for the inmate population of particular establishments. Sub-groups of the prison population that are granted HDC less often than average tend to have higher than average risk scores, suggesting that the risk assessment process is working largely as planned. However, it is also possible that some variation is as a result of the different approaches to HDC implementation and assessment taken by Prison Service Area Managers and local governors. There is less variation in rates of recall to prison.

Women are more likely to be granted HDC than men (40% of eligible prisoners compared with 29% for male prisoners), reflecting their lower average risk of reoffending and reimprisonment. In general, older prisoners are more likely to be granted HDC than younger ones. Black prisoners are marginally more likely than white to be granted HDC (31% compared to 29%), but South Asian (51%) and Chinese & Other (39%) inmates are much more likely to be released early onto the scheme. Again, these release rates are closely linked to actuarial risk assessments and reflect what also happens in parole decisions (see Hood and Shute, 2000).

Analysis of the release rates onto HDC by different offence types again confirms the importance of risk in these decisions. Offenders convicted of offences with higher reconviction rates, such as burglary and theft & handling, have lower HDC release rates, while the opposite is true for drugs offences and fraud & forgery – these offences have lower reconviction rates and higher release rates.

The rate of recall to prison from HDC has remained more or less constant over the first 16 months of the scheme, at around five per cent. There is no clear link between establishments' release rates and recall rates – that is, those prisons that release a higher proportion of eligible inmates onto HDC are not associated with higher levels of recall following a breakdown of the curfew. Recalls were highest for those convicted of burglary (10%) compared to just two per cent for those convicted of fraud and forgery.

The views of curfewees

The generally successful operation of HDC was confirmed by the survey of curfewees, family members and supervising probation officers, suggesting that the scheme has had some success in achieving its aim of easing the transition from custody into the community. Respondents did, however, identify some areas where the scheme might be improved.

Curfewees were very positive about the scheme, with only two per cent saying that they would have preferred to spend the time in prison rather than on HDC. Prior to release, over a third of prisoners (37%) said that the prospect of being granted HDC influenced their behaviour in prison. Other household members were also very positive about the scheme. Probation officers supervising those curfewees subject to non-HDC licences (in addition to the curfew) were also generally in favour of HDC and felt that it supported their work with the curfewee.

While the majority of curfewees interviewed (83%) remembered being given something in writing with the rules of the scheme, less than one in three (29%) had seen the video about the scheme. Almost half (49%) felt that they were quite, or very poorly informed about the scheme prior to release.

According to the curfewees themselves, the main advantages of the scheme were being out of prison (82%) and meeting up with family. Other household members said that the main advantages were having the curfewee back home (72%) and no more need for prison visits (69%). Neither group mentioned many disadvantages, although 41 per cent of curfewees cited the curfew restrictions as a disadvantage.

At the time of interview, one-third of curfewees were in work (28% full-time, 6% part-time), with a further 36 per cent seeking work. This latter group was most likely to cite advantages (such as developing a routine and enabling them to look for work) and also more likely than others to cite disadvantages (such as the difficulty of finding a job because of the curfew restrictions and the inconvenience of the curfew hours for other household members).

Sixty-one per cent of curfewees said they had experienced a curfew violation.[1] Nearly two-thirds of these claimed that the violation was down to equipment failure rather than any action (or inaction) on their own part. However, neither the electronic monitoring contractors, the Home Office nor the Prison Service had become aware of any widespread equipment malfunction. The staff of the monitoring companies were praised by curfewees and household members as being polite, helpful and professional, especially at the installation, though also when dealing with violations. (Even where these violations were confirmed by the monitoring staff, they were not sufficiently serious to warrant recall to prison at that stage.)

A small sub-sample of recalled prisoners was also interviewed to discover the factors underlying their breaches of the curfew conditions. Broadly, there were four main categories that caused either violations or recalls, some of which overlapped.

Equipment problems
Some of those interviewed claimed that problems with the equipment lay behind their recall. Visits by monitoring staff to check on violations and/or equipment had also resulted in threatening behaviour by one curfewee who was then recalled on those grounds.

Psychological issues
Motivation was a key issue for many, with a number of those interviewed lacking the discipline required to keep to the curfew. Some had experienced problems following a return to drug use or to a criminal lifestyle that they had known prior to prison. Anger management also caused problems for some and arguments with other members of the household or with the monitoring staff could lead (directly or indirectly) to recall.

Housing and domestic issues
Problems with unsuitable housing or unstable tenure were a factor in some of those interviewed being recalled to prison. Relationship problems were often associated with either a loss of accommodation or curfew violations. Family support was also an important factor in a curfewee's ability to cope on HDC. Isolation and boredom were particular problems for those living by themselves.

---

1   "Curfew violation" means that the curfewee broke the rules of the curfew. The question was worded so as to ask curfewees if they had experienced a violation, regardless of whether they felt that they had actually infringed the rules. In addition to cases where there was an acknowledged breaking of the curfew rules, responses would therefore also pick up cases where the curfewee felt that there had been no violation but s/he was contacted by the monitoring companies in relation to an alleged violation.

Lifestyle

The need to be available to work shifts, long hours or to do overtime, especially at short notice, can conflict with the curfew requirements. This can also make it harder for some curfewees to find or take work. On the other hand, some of the recalled prisoners interviewed were characterised by a hedonistic lifestyle and once released went back to the largely nocturnal activities of pubs and clubs, disregarding the requirements of the curfew. The impact of drug and alcohol use on the ability to keep to curfew times or other licence conditions also led to some recalls.

Most of the recalled curfewees interviewed said that the lure of "freedom" on HDC was very strong and made it less likely that those being assessed would be realistic about the chances of their completing the curfew period. This, coupled with the high numbers who felt poorly informed, suggests that more could be done to inform and prepare prisoners both before and during the assessment process so that they understand some of the pressures that they will face and have a chance to think about how to cope with them.

Three-quarters of all respondents had been in contact with the probation service since release. Of these, two-thirds described their meetings as "generally helpful". Probation officers were also positive, with just under a quarter (23%) saying it helped their work with a named curfewee a lot and a fifth (20%) saying it helped their work a little. (Most of the remainder – 53% of the total – felt that it made no difference.) Furthermore, in *general* terms (i.e. not related to a specific case), 76 per cent of probation officers interviewed felt that HDC helped their work.

Cost-benefit analysis of HDC

A key part of the evaluation has been an analysis of the financial costs and benefits of Home Detention Curfew over the first year of the scheme. This involved identifying the main costs in each of the main HDC processes: risk assessment; contractor operations; and recalls. This included estimating the actual resource cost to prisons and probation services of carrying out the assessments and to the Sentence Enforcement Unit in making decisions on recalls (e.g. the time spent on HDC duties and the grades of the different staff involved in the process).

The average period spent on HDC was 45 days, at a cost of approximately £1,300 per curfew (equivalent to £880 per month) which contributes to a resource saving over the year of £63.4 million. The scheme had a net effect of reducing the prison population by around 1,950 prison places over the first 12 months of operation (the average number of curfewees at any one time in this period) and will continue to save places.

The biggest costs by far were payments made to the electronic monitoring contractors, while the main driver for savings was the reduction in prison places. The total estimated net benefit of the Home Detention Curfew scheme over the first year was £36.7 million (this excludes start-up costs for all but the electronic monitoring contractors). This does not represent a reduction of £36.7 million in Prison Service cash flows as the Service still has to run the existing establishments. However, at a time when the prison population was rising, it helped reduce the need for capital expenditure on new prisons.[2]

The costs and benefits of Home Detention Curfew are summarised in Table 2.

Table 2:   Costs and benefits of Home Detention Curfew over the first 12 months

Agency	Estimated Cost	Estimated Benefit
Prison staff costs	£3.2m	
Probation service costs	£2.3m	
Contractor costs (actual charges made ex. VAT)	£21.0m	
Sentence Enforcement Unit	£0.15m	
Prison resource savings		£63.4m
Net benefits		£36.7m[3]
Prison places saved		1950

Analysis of reoffending

One of the key concerns has been whether HDC has had any impact on reconvictions. A short-term reconviction analysis was carried out on a sample of prisoners who were eligible for discharge on HDC in May and June 1999, some of whom were released on HDC and some of whom were not. This programme group was compared with a control group of similar discharged prisoners taken from October and November 1998 who would have been eligible for consideration for HDC had it been in force at the time. Data on short-term reconvictions (up to six months after the automatic release date)[4] were analysed for both groups using Police National Computer (PNC) conviction data.

---

2   The Prison Service Annual Report and Accounts for 1999–2000 quotes an overcrowding rate (prisoners held two to a cell designed for one) of 18.9%.
3   Not including start-up costs, except for the monitoring contractors.
4   This is the date on which they would have been discharged anyway, had they been refused HDC.

Just over two per cent (2.1%) of curfewees were reconvicted for offences committed while subject to HDC. In the six months after the curfew period or discharge date, offenders eligible for HDC had very similar reconviction rates to the control group (30.5% and 30.0% respectively, or 30.8% and 30.0% if offences during the curfew period are included). The differences between the programme group and the control group were not statistically significant. This suggests that the impact of HDC is broadly neutral in terms of reoffending when compared with the results for the control group. The analysis provides further evidence that the risk assessment process is effective: of those granted HDC, the reconviction rate for the six month period after their automatic release date was 9.3 per cent, compared with a rate of 40.5 per cent of those who were refused HDC.

There is also evidence that the risk assessment is operated effectively not only at the aggregate level, but also for individuals. Curfewees with a high actuarial risk of reoffending actually had *lower* than predicted reconviction rates, which suggests that HDC staff in prisons and probation services are using their professional judgement effectively.

Conclusions

In general, Home Detention Curfew appears to be operating relatively smoothly and has gone some of the way to achieving its central aim of easing the transition from custody to the community. Furthermore, this has been achieved at the same time as realising significant cost savings and with very little impact on reoffending.

1.   Introduction

The Home Detention Curfew (HDC) scheme was announced to the House of Commons by the Home Secretary, Jack Straw, in November 1997, and formed part of what became the Crime and Disorder Act, 1998. The scheme was intended primarily to ease the transition of prisoners from custody to the community by allowing suitable inmates to be released up to two months before their normal release date, provided that they comply with an electronically monitored curfew for that period.

Home Detention Curfew came into force on 28 January 1999 and was implemented nationally from that date, becoming one of the largest electronic monitoring schemes in the world. In all, some 16,000 prisoners were placed on HDC during its first year of operation and this evaluation focuses largely on that period.

With a few statutory exceptions, those prisoners serving a sentence of three months or more and less than four years are eligible to be considered for HDC. Those who pass a risk and suitability assessment and who have suitable accommodation are released by the prison and are tagged by the relevant electronic monitoring contractors who then monitor compliance with the terms of the HDC licence.

For the purposes of organising the monitoring, England and Wales has been divided into four HDC regions. Electronic monitoring services are provided by three contractor companies: Securicor Custodial Services covers the Northern region; Premier Monitoring Services covers the Midlands & Wales and London & Eastern regions; and GSSC covers the Southern region.

If an offender fails to comply with the curfew and this is considered to be sufficiently serious, either by itself or in conjunction with other violations of the curfew rules, the details are forwarded to the Sentence Enforcement Unit at the Prison Service who decide whether the breach is genuine. If the breach is confirmed, the curfewee will be recalled: s/he will be picked up by the police and taken by the custody escort service to the nearest suitable prison establishment to serve the remaining part of their custodial sentence. Prisoners recalled in such a way have a right of appeal against the decision to recall.

Background to the scheme

As mentioned above, the decision to set up the Home Detention Curfew scheme was announced in late 1997 and implemented across the whole of England and Wales from 28 January 1999. Prior to this an extensive bidding exercise had been undertaken for awarding the electronic monitoring contracts.

First, a range of companies were invited to express interest. From those who responded, a shortlist of four was drawn up who were invited to submit tenders detailing their proposed monitoring operation and pricing schedule. These bids were assessed against the Home Office's operational requirements and subsequently three preferred bidders were selected: Securicor Custodial Services for the Northern region, GSSC for the Southern region, and Premier Monitoring Services for the London & Eastern and Midlands & Wales regions. Following post-tender negotiations, the companies set up their monitoring centres and recruited and trained staff. Before the scheme went live, each of the companies had to pass acceptance tests to establish that the staff and equipment were capable of carrying out the necessary tasks.

While Home Detention Curfew has quickly become one of the largest electronic monitoring schemes in the world, it builds on a decade of experience in electronic monitoring in England and Wales. The generally successful implementation of the scheme owed much to the work of all the agencies and individuals involved, but was also based on a good deal of experience of using electronic monitoring in criminal justice systems both at home and abroad.

Overview of the report

This report brings together the various strands of the evaluation. Chapter 2 gives an overview of how the scheme operates. The main parts of the evaluation are contained in Chapters 3 to 6. Chapter 3 contains analyses of numbers eligible, numbers released, curfew completions and recalls. The surveys of curfewees both on curfew and following recall, of their families and supervising probation officers are reported in Chapter 4. Chapter 5 contains an analysis of the costs and benefits of the HDC scheme and Chapter 6 contains a study of reconvictions of offenders while on HDC and subsequent to the curfew period. Chapter 7 draws together conclusions from the evaluation of HDC.

Methodology and data sources

A variety of research methods and data sources have been used in the preparation of this report. Data on eligible populations, release rates and recalls have come from the Prison Service's Inmate Information System.

The research company RSGB was commissioned to carry out quantitative face-to-face interview surveys of curfewees and their families, telephone interviews with curfewees' supervising probation officers, and qualitative interviews with a smaller sample of curfewees recalled to prison following breach or other breakdown of the curfew.

The reconviction study utilises data from the Police National Computer, and compares a control group of offenders released prior to the start of the HDC scheme (who would otherwise have been eligible) with samples taken after the start of the scheme (including both those who were placed on HDC and those who were turned down for the scheme).

The data on costs were taken, where available, from existing official sources. However, information was not available on the precise costs on prisons of carrying out the new HDC work, so this was obtained by carrying out an activity recording exercise in a range of prisons.

2.   An overview of the Home Detention Curfew scheme

In order for an offender to be released on Home Detention Curfew (HDC), s/he must fit the eligibility criteria and also pass a risk assessment carried out by the prison and the home probation service. This assessment is designed to ascertain the prisoner's suitability for the scheme, and whether the home circumstances are suitable. This chapter details how this process operates and what happens to prisoners after release.

Eligibility

Those eligible for HDC are prisoners aged 18 or over serving a sentence of three months or more but less than four years. Some categories of prisoner are not eligible for the scheme, such as those required to register under the Sex Offenders Act, 1997, fine defaulters, those awaiting deportation and those breached for failing to comply with a curfew order with electronic monitoring or who have previously been breached for non-compliance with HDC.

The assessment process

Although a prisoner may be eligible for Home Detention Curfew they will not be released unless they pass a risk assessment carried out by the prison and home probation service. The assessment attempts to determine the likelihood of the prisoner's reoffending whilst on the scheme, and of his/her complying with the curfew conditions. The assessment process has a number of stages:

- an assessment of initial suitability by the prison
- outside probation assessment of home circumstances
- assessment by seconded probation team/authorised officer
- enhanced assessment
- governor's authorisation.

The outside probation assessment and the enhanced assessment are not carried out for all prisoners. These and the other stages will now be described in more detail, along with the timetable for completing the HDC assessment.

The HDC assessment timetable

The role of Prison Service establishments in the HDC assessment process is detailed in Prison Service Order (PSO) 6700 (chapter 5, page 2). This is reproduced in Table 2.1.

Table 2.1: *Home Detention Curfew assessment timetable*

Timing	Action
Post sentence	Prisoner encouraged to address offending behaviour and to locate suitable accommodation
Ten weeks before HDC eligibility date (HDCED)	(i) Prisoner completes form HDC2, giving details of his/her proposed address (ii) Member of prison staff's comments to be entered in part 2 of HDC1 form
Nine weeks before HDCED	Initial read-through of papers
Eight weeks prior to HDCED	HDC3 (or PD1) form sent to home probation service for return within ten working days
Five weeks prior to HDCED	HDC1 form completed
Three weeks prior to HDCED	HDC4 form completed if required
Two weeks prior to HDCED	Prisoner (and where required, other agencies) to be informed of decision on HDC
HDCED	If approved for HDC, prisoner released on HDC

The initial suitability assessment for eligible prisoners

The prison carries out an initial suitability assessment of the prisoner for HDC. Initially, the prisoner is asked to give details of their proposed curfew address and any other residents living at that address (using the HDC2 form). If the prisoner does not have an address then s/he will not be eligible for HDC and no further assessment will take place. The prisoner can also decline to be considered for HDC.

An appropriate member of the prison staff with regular day-to-day contact with the prisoner (e.g. the prisoner's personal officer or an officer on the prisoner's wing) provides information on any factors relating to the prisoner's suitability for HDC. These factors include whether s/he has had a successful history of Release on Temporary Licence (ROTL), any progress s/he has made in addressing offending behaviour and the prisoner's attitude and behaviour in custody. This information is written on the HDC1 form. Also noted on the HDC1 form are the prisoner's risk prediction scores (i.e. the statistical probability of an offender committing a sexual, violent or other offence within two years of release, or of being reimprisoned within the same period).

A probation officer based in the establishment (or another authorised HDC officer) then conducts an initial scrutiny of the documents available (e.g. pre-sentence reports, previous-convictions, risk predictor scores, etc.) to determine whether there are any immediate issues which the prison staff or home probation service should be invited to comment on. If relevant (for example, if there is doubt about a prisoner's mental health), prison healthcare staff may also be consulted.

Probation service assessment of home circumstances

Input from the home probation service should only be requested by the prison if the inmate has a *realistic* chance of getting HDC. The home probation service assesses the suitability of the proposed curfew address, and if possible, provides information on domestic circumstances, victim issues and the suitability of the prisoner for HDC. The prison can request the probation service to comment on other particular issues. The probation service completes their assessment using an HDC3 form which is returned to the prison.

Assessment by seconded probation team/authorised officer

Either the establishment's seconded probation officer or other authorised officer then completes the HDC1 form by summarising the prisoner's suitability for HDC. This summary must cover a review of the prisoner's core documentation (e.g. pre-sentence report, previous convictions, sentence plan), the reports by prison staff, the probation service comments (if obtained) and the prisoner's risk prediction scores.

The officer must make a recommendation for or against release based on the evidence they have summarised. They can then either refer the inmate to the authorising Governor for consideration for HDC or refer the inmate for an enhanced assessment. If the inmate is referred to the authorising Governor at this stage, the Governor can either agree to release the prisoner on HDC or if they are unsure they can refer the case back for an enhanced assessment.

Enhanced assessment

A case should only be referred to an enhanced board if:

- the risk prediction scores indicate that the prisoner is in the statistically high risk category for reconviction for sex offences, violent offences, or for reimprisonment
- the offender is serving over one year and does not have a successful history of release on temporary licence
- the evidence collected suggests that there is a legitimate case for not releasing the prisoner on HDC.

The enhanced assessment must be completed by a board consisting of at least a Governor grade and a seconded probation officer or a member of the throughcare team. If available a member of the prison staff with regular contact with the prisoner should also attend. However, due to short sentences, time spent on remand, prisoners being transferred in from other establishments for short periods of time, prisoners being moved from wing to wing and staff shortages there is very often not a member of staff who knows the prisoner well.

The board must consider the HDC1 form and core documents. They must consider in particular: previous criminal history; participation in and response to offending behaviour work in prison; release on temporary licence; relevant behaviour in prison (e.g. whether there have been any adjudications against the prisoner); likelihood of reoffending or breaching curfew conditions; and home circumstances. The chair of the board will complete the HDC4 form recording the board's decision and the reasons for it. The recommendation is then referred to the authorising Governor who makes the final decision.

Governor's authorisation

The final decision whether to grant HDC or not must be taken by an authorised Governor on behalf of the Secretary of State. The main governor is authorised to take the decision on behalf of the Secretary of State but may delegate the task to a Governor of grade 4 or above if the area manager approves. This is usually what happens and means that the main governor is free to deal with any appeals against a decision to refuse HDC.

The prisoner is then informed of the outcome of their HDC application. If they are successful the prison notifies the relevant agencies (i.e. the monitoring contractor, the home probation service and the National Identification Service) of the prisoner's release. If HDC is refused, the prisoner can appeal formally to the main governor and, if successful, s/he will be released.

The curfew

The maximum period of the curfew is 60 days and the minimum is normally 14 days. The length of the curfew will depend on the length of a prisoner's custodial sentence. The place and times of the curfew are set by the prison governor. This must be for a minimum of nine hours a day and, in most cases, will be for 12 hours a day lasting from early evening to early morning. Curfews longer than 12 hours a day may only be imposed if it is likely to increase the probability of the curfew being completed successfully, for example, if it prohibits the offender from being out when it is known that they are particularly likely to be vulnerable to the availability of alcohol.

Monitoring

Private sector contractors are responsible for monitoring offenders and notifying the prison service if the offender breaches their curfew conditions. As noted in Chapter 1, there are three monitoring companies covering England and Wales:

- Securicor Custodial Services covers the Northern region
- Premier Monitoring Services covers the Midlands & Wales and London & Eastern regions
- GSSC covers the Southern region.

The contractors fit a Personal Identification Device (PID or tag), usually to the offender's ankle, or to the wrist in certain circumstances. This PID communicates electronically with a monitoring unit. The monitoring unit is installed in the offender's home, and is calibrated to detect whether the PID which has been fitted to the offender is at the place of curfew. The monitoring unit is connected to the telephone line through which it communicates with a central computer system. This notifies the monitoring staff of any infringements of the curfew hours or any attempt to interfere with the monitoring equipment. If the computer system does detect a violation, the contractors telephone the offender and if necessary make a home visit to confirm that a violation has occurred. Once confirmed, the contractors may issue a warning to the offender or, if the violation is serious enough (either by itself or in conjunction with previous violations), contact the Sentence Enforcement Unit of the Prison Service, who will decide whether to amend or revoke the licence (violations are discussed further in the recall section).

The Probation Service is responsible for post-release supervision of Automatic Conditional Release (ACR) prisoners (i.e. prisoners sentenced to 12 months or more in custody) and all young offenders, as laid down in the Home Office's National Standards for the Supervision of Offenders in the Community. If an ACR prisoner or young offender is released on HDC, his/her post-release supervision is brought forward, starting the same time as the HDC period. (The post-release supervision period does not increase because the offender is on HDC, it simply ends earlier than it would have done if the prisoner had been released on his/her ACR date.) Apart from the period of supervision being brought forward, HDC has little effect on post-release supervision. Prisoners serving less than 12 months (Automatic Unconditional Release) are not subject to any post-release supervision by the probation service.

Recalls

Unauthorised absences from the place of curfew during the curfew period, tampering with the equipment and violence (or threats of violence) against the contactors' staff are violations. There are different levels of violations, and the most serious (or an accumulation of less serious violations) can result in a breach of the curfew. Following a breach, the contractors submit a report to the Sentence Enforcement Unit, who then decide whether to amend or revoke the licence. A confirmed breach will normally lead to a revocation of the HDC licence and the prisoner will be returned to custody where (subject to any appeal) they will serve the remainder of their sentence up to their automatic or conditional release date.

The HDC licence can also be amended or revoked if it is no longer possible to monitor the whereabouts of the curfewee, if it is considered that the curfewee poses a risk of serious harm to the public or if the curfewee is charged with an offence committed whilst on HDC. ACR curfewees who committed their original offence on or after 1 January 1999 can also be recalled under separate powers for breaches of the non-HDC part of their licence. If an offender is charged with a new offence while on HDC, the police are required to notify the Sentence Enforcement Unit so that they can recall the curfewee.

Once the Sentence Enforcement Unit has confirmed a breach and decided to recall the curfewee, the police are notified and the record on the Police National Computer is amended to reflect this. The police then should pick up the offender and hold him/her until s/he is picked up by the custody escort service and taken to the nearest suitable prison establishment.

Appeals

If a curfewee is recalled s/he can appeal against the decision. There are three possible outcomes of an appeal: (a) the decision to recall can be upheld, (b) the decision to recall can be overturned and (c) the reason for recall can be changed. If the curfewee is recalled because they have breached their curfew conditions then they are not eligible for HDC in future. In some cases the reason for recall is recorded as a breach of curfew conditions where in fact the offender was not at fault (e.g. the recall was due to an installation or monitoring failure). In cases such as these the offender may appeal to and have the reason for recall changed so that they will be eligible for HDC should they be imprisoned at some time in the future.

3.

Home Detention Curfew – the first sixteen months of operation

This chapter begins with an overview of the numbers eligible to be considered for Home Detention Curfew and released in the first 16 months of the scheme (28 January 1999 to 31 May 2000) and then examines release and recall rates by sex, age, ethnicity, offence type, sentence length, establishment, prison area and HDC region.

In the first 16 months of operation, 72,400 prisoners (approximately 4,500 a month) were eligible to be considered for Home Detention Curfew and, of those, just under 21,400 prisoners (approximately 1,300 a month) were released after passing the risk assessment carried out by prison and probation staff (a release rate of 30%).[1] On average, approximately 2,000 prisoners were on Home Detention Curfew at any one time and the average length of the curfew was 45 days. Although the majority of prisoners completed their curfew successfully, just over 1,100 of the 21,400 prisoners released on the scheme were recalled to custody by the Prison Service acting on behalf of the Secretary of State (a recall rate of 5%). Table 3.1 summarises the key data for the first 16 months of operation.

Table 3.1: HDC data for the first 16 months of operation

Total number of prison population discharged	126,400
Numbers eligible to be considered for HDC	72,400
Eligibility rate (as percentage of discharged population)	57%
Numbers released on HDC	21,400
Release rate (as percentage of those eligible)	30%
Number recalled	1,100
Recall rate (as percentage of those placed on HDC)	5%
Average number on curfew at any one time	2,000

Note: all figures are rounded to the nearest 100

---

1   For each eligible prisoner the prison should record the assessment process on the Local Inmate Data System documenting the stages of the assessment, the outcome (i.e. granted or not granted) and the reasons for that decision. Unfortunately, the assessment record is incomplete for 26 per cent of prisoners assessed. It seems that if a prisoner is refused HDC their assessment record is often left incomplete. It has therefore not been possible to carry out any analysis of HDC assessments.

There are a number of reasons why a prisoner could be recalled to prison from HDC (see Figure 3.1). The most common reason for recall was breach of curfew conditions – accounting for two-thirds of all recalls (68%). This category includes being absent from the curfew address, threatening monitoring staff, damaging the equipment or failing to be present for the installation of a new telephone line or equipment. Only eight curfewees out of approximately 1,100 were recalled on the grounds that they represented a risk of serious harm to the public.

A number of prisoners were recalled on the grounds that it was not possible to monitor them. These fell into three categories: 'change of circumstances', 'installation failure' and 'monitoring failure'. Curfewees recalled on the basis of a 'change in circumstances' (for example, where they involuntarily lost their curfew address or withdrew their consent to be monitored) accounted for 25 per cent of all recalls. 'Installation failure' (where it was not possible to install the monitoring equipment or make the monitoring equipment fully operational) and 'monitoring failure' (where it became impossible to continue monitoring, for technical or other reasons) accounted for one per cent and two per cent of recalls respectively. The remaining three per cent of curfewees were recalled for breaking general non-HDC licence conditions[2] (see Figure 3.1).

Figure 3.1: Reasons for recall in the first 16 months of operation

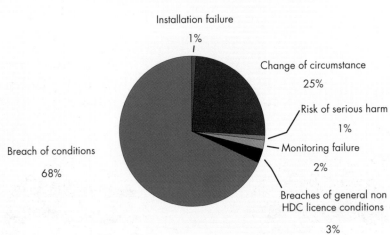

Installation failure
1%

Change of circumstance
25%

Risk of serious harm
1%

Monitoring failure
2%

Breaches of general non HDC licence conditions
3%

Breach of conditions
68%

Of the 1,100 prisoners released onto HDC in the first 16 months of the scheme and subsequently recalled to prison, 210 appealed against the decision to recall. For 188 (90%) of these, the decision to recall was upheld and for 22 (10%) the decision was overturned. When the decision to recall is overturned the prisoner can be re-released on HDC if there is

2   Prisoners serving sentences of 12 months or more are subject to supervision up to the three-quarters point of sentence and licence conditions which are independent of Home Detention Curfew.

enough of his/her curfew period left. Thirteen cases (7% of appeals) for whom the decision to recall was upheld were allowed to have the reason for recall changed. If a prisoner is recalled to custody for breaching the curfew conditions, s/he is not eligible for HDC in the future. By having the reason for recall amended to change of circumstances, installation failure or monitoring failure, the recalled prisoner becomes eligible to be considered for HDC should s/he be reimprisoned in future.

Variations in releases and recalls

Contractor areas – HDC releases and recalls

Three private sector electronic monitoring contractors are responsible for monitoring curfewees in four HDC areas across England and Wales. The Northern region is monitored by Securicor Custodial Services, the Southern region by GSSC and the Midlands & Wales and London & Eastern regions are covered by Premier Monitoring Services. Thirty-one per cent of eligible prisoners were released onto HDC in the Northern region, 29 per cent in Midlands & Wales, 24 per cent in London & Eastern regions and 16 per cent in the Southern region. The number of recalls in each area was proportionate to the number of curfewees monitored, suggesting that prisoners have been recalled at a similar rate in each region (see Figure 3.2).

Figure 3.2 **Proportion of persons on HDC in the first 16 months of operation in each area** **Proportion of persons recalled to prison from HDC in each area**

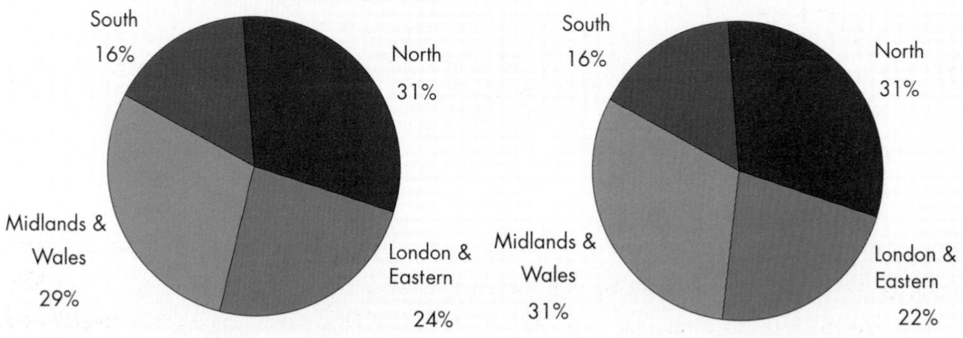

South 16%
North 31%
Midlands & Wales 29%
London & Eastern 24%

South 16%
North 31%
Midlands & Wales 31%
London & Eastern 22%

Prison areas: HDC release and recall rates

The release rate varies quite dramatically between Prison Service areas: Kent, Surrey and Sussex had the highest release rate at 43 per cent and Mersey, Manchester and Cheshire had the lowest release rate at 15 per cent (see Figure 3.3). This variation is likely to be related to the different mix of establishments and prisoner populations, i.e. some areas may contain more establishments which house 'higher' risk prisoners and therefore are more likely to have low release rates onto HDC. This is illustrated by the High Security Estate having one of the lowest HDC release rates and the Female Estate having one of the highest (on average female prisoners tend to be at lower risk of reconviction than males and have a higher HDC release rate). The variation may also be a result of different attitudes of Prison Service Area Managers and governors regarding appropriate levels of risk. It is important to note, however, that release rates vary quite dramatically within Prison Service areas as well as between them, i.e. not all establishments in Mersey, Manchester and Cheshire have low release rates. The recall rate only varied between three per cent and six per cent across prison areas and was not necessarily related to the release rate (see Figure 3.3).

Figure 3.3   HDC release and recall rates by prison area

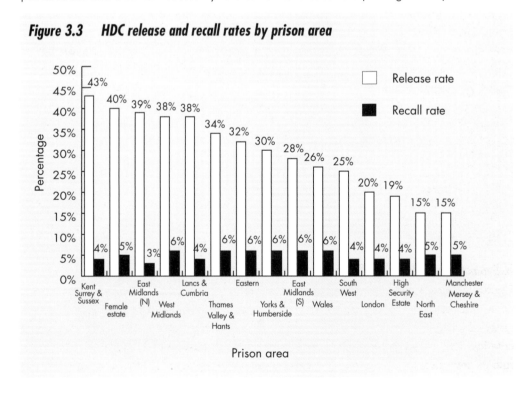

Establishment types: HDC release and recall rates

Open prisons and open Young Offender Institutions contain lower risk prisoners and have relatively high release rates onto HDC. Conversely, prisons containing higher risk prisoners, such as closed training establishments and closed Young Offenders Institutions have lower release rates, as shown in Figure 3.4. This is in line with what would be expected, and reflects the role of the risk assessment in determining whether a prisoner is placed on HDC. Local prisons have a lower release rate and this is partly due to their holding prisoners serving very short sentences, where there may be insufficient time to complete a suitability assessment. Release rates also vary between establishments of the same type. This may partly be explained by the different types of offender they are holding (even prisons of the same category can hold very different types of offender), but is probably also related to the way HDC has been implemented in the prison. Recall rates also vary between types of establishment from one per cent for open prisons (which hold lower-risk inmates and release more prisoners on HDC) to ten per cent for local prisons (see Figure 3.4).

Figure 3.4: HDC release and recall rates by type of establishment

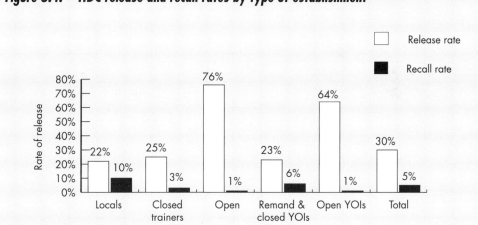

Individual establishments: HDC release and recall rates

Figure 3.5 plots each establishment's release rate by its recall rate. It suggests that there is no obvious relationship between release and recall rates. If establishments housed the same types of prisoners with the same level of risk and applied exactly the same assessment criteria, then one might expect two establishments releasing prisoners onto HDC at the same rate to have similar rates of recall. However, as mentioned earlier, prisons will differ in the level of risk in their population, so one prison's released population will contain higher risk inmates than might be found in another establishment. In addition, prisons are likely to differ in the effectiveness of their suitability assessments, which may influence their level of recall.

The degree to which these factors affect variations in release and recall rates across establishments is as yet undetermined and it is likely that numerous other factors will have an impact (e.g. the number of short term prisoners held in the establishment, resources and time available to deal with the risk assessment process, the size of the prison population, etc.). It is also important to acknowledge that the number of recalls are so low that any variations across individual establishments are not likely to be statistically significant.[3]

Figure 3.5:   Establishments' HDC release rates by recall rates

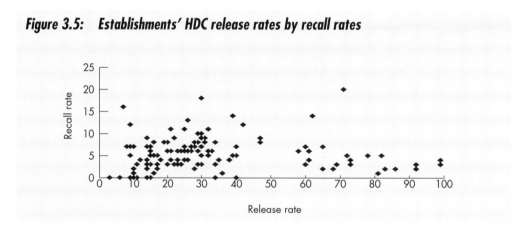

Sex: HDC release and recall rates
Women constitute a higher proportion of the HDC eligible population (7%) than of the prison population (5%) and an even higher proportion of those released onto HDC (9%). The rate of release for women prisoners was 40 per cent, compared with 29 per cent for male prisoners. This is likely to be connected with the fact that women tend to have lower reconviction rates which will be reflected in the HDC risk assessment. There was no difference in the proportion of males and females recalled to prisons; five per cent of both men and women were recalled.

Ethnic group: HDC release and recall rates
There is very little difference between the HDC release rate for white (29%) and black (31%) offenders. However, South Asian offenders have a significantly higher release rate at 51 per cent, and the release rate for Chinese and other groups is also higher than average at 39 per cent (see Figure 3.6).[4] The higher release rate for South Asians is likely to be related to

---

3   Figure 3.5 does not indicate the numbers being released, only the rates. One example is the most obvious outlying establishment in the Figure, with a release rate of 71 per cent and a recall rate of 20 per cent which only had 14 eligible inmates in this period, of whom 10 were released and two subsequently recalled.

4   Only 2,000 South Asian prisoners and 2,000 Chinese and other prisoners were eligible for HDC compared to 5,500 Black prisoners and 63,500 White prisoners. This is because South Asian prisoners and Chinese and other prisoners only constitute a small proportion of the general prison population – three per cent each (see Prison Statistics England and Wales, 1999).

the types of offences committed by this group of prisoners, their behaviour in prison and their overall lower reconviction rates. South Asian, Chinese and other prisoners also have a lower recall rate than black and white prisoners. The recall rate is two per cent for South Asian prisoners and three per cent for Chinese and other prisoners compared to five per cent for black and white prisoners (these differences may not be statistically significant due to small numbers).

Figure 3.6:   HDC release and recall rates by ethnic group

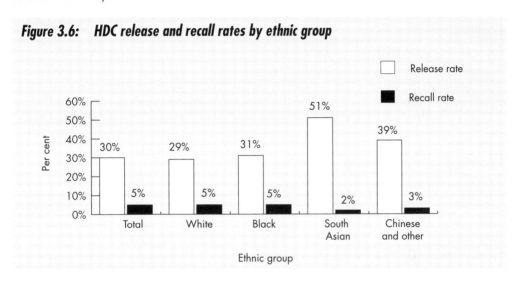

Age: HDC release and recall rates

The release rate onto HDC tends to increase with the age of the prisoner (see Figure 3.7). However, those aged 60 and over are an exception – the release rate is lower for this group than for those aged 40 to 59. However, numbers in the oldest age group are relatively low and the release rate is still much higher than the average. The increasing release rate with age is likely to be associated with the higher risk of reconviction for younger age bands.

Figure 3.7: HDC release and recall rates by age

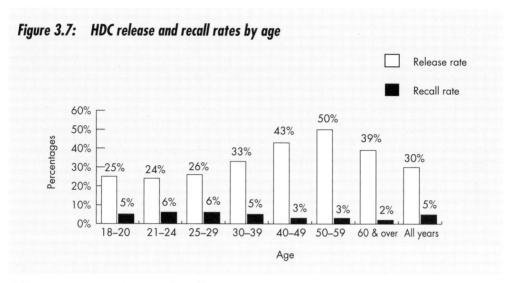

Offence type: HDC release and recall rates

The release rate by type of offence varies markedly from the average rate of 30 per cent. This variation in release rates is related to the reconviction rates across different offence types. Figure 3.8 compares the percentage of prisoners discharged in 1996 who were reconvicted within two years with the HDC release rates for those offences. The release rate for offence types declines as the reconviction rates rise, i.e. those prisoners convicted of an offence where there is a high probability of reconviction are less likely to be placed on HDC. However, there is one exception: although the reconviction rate for sex offenders is low, so is the release rate. This is because offenders required to register under the Sex Offenders Act 1997 were not eligible to be released on the scheme *"save in exceptional circumstances and with the approval of the Director General of the Prison Service"*.[5] Recall rates also vary by offence type (see Table 3.2). The offence with the lowest recall rate (apart from sex offences) was fraud and forgery at two per cent, while the offence with the highest recall rate was burglary at ten per cent. Sex offenders had a recall rate of zero per cent as very few were released.

---

5   Home Office, Home Detention Curfew Information Protocol, version 1/99, page 2. The provisions of the Criminal Justice and Court Services Act, 2000, have now closed the possibility of any offender who is required to register under the Sex Offenders Act (1997) being released on HDC.

Figure 3.8:   HDC release rates and reconviction rates by offence type

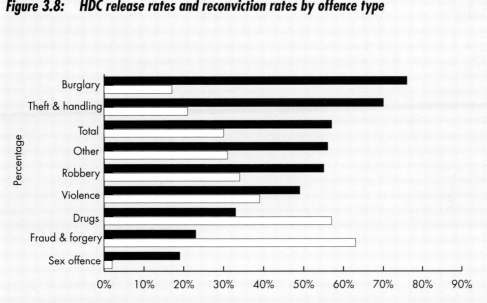

Note: The reconviction rates are the percentage of prisoners released in 1995 from prison who were reconvicted of a further offence within two years (Kershaw et al., 1999). The reconviction rates cover all prisoners, not just those serving three months or more but less than four years.

Table 3.2:   HDC recall rates by offence type

	Released [1]	Recall rate
Sexual	0	0%
Fraud and forgery	1,800	2%
Drugs	3,500	3%
Violence	3,800	4%
Theft and handling	2,900	5%
Robbery	900	7%
Burglary	2,000	10%
Other	6,500	5%
Total	21,400	5%

1   Releases are rounded to the nearest 100.

Sentence length: HDC release and recall rates

The release rate onto HDC Release tends to increase as the length of sentence increases (see Figure 3.9). As the length of sentence is likely to reflect the seriousness of the offence, one might expect this pattern to go in the opposite direction (i.e. the longer the sentence, the lower the release rate). However, the lower release rate for shorter sentences can probably be explained by the tight timescales with which prisons and probation have to work when assessing a prisoner's suitability for HDC. The pressure is increased when account is taken of time spent on remand and of transfers between prisons during the sentence. The recall rate also rises as the sentence length increases which may be related to the fact that the longer sentence lengths have a longer time on curfew. Table 3.3 compares the original length of curfew with the time spent on curfew before recall for prisoners who were recalled to prison.

Figure 3.9: HDC release and recall rates by sentence length

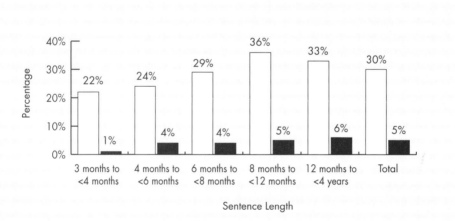

Recalls: a comparison of the original length of curfew with the time spent on curfew before recall

Table 3.3 shows the original curfew length of recalled prisoners by the actual length of time spent on HDC before recall. The majority of recalled prisoners, 562 (53%), had a curfew period of between 57 and 60 days. Few curfewees were likely to be recalled to prison by the Prison Service in the last week of their curfew period (unsurprisingly, this is less true for prisoners who only had a curfew period of 0 to 14 days). For most curfew lengths, prisoners tended to be recalled in the first couple of weeks of their curfew, although this was less true for the prisoners with a curfew length of 57 to 60 days for whom recalls were more evenly spread across the whole curfew period.

Table 3.3   Original length of curfew by actual time spent on curfew for recalled prisoners

Time spent on curfew before recall	Original length of curfew								
	0–14 days	15–21 days	22–28 days	29–35 days	36–42 days	43–49 days	50–56 days	57–60 days	Total
0–7 days	53%	50%	43%	36%	22%	23%	26%	12%	21%
8–14 days	47%	40%	30%	16%	25%	25%	21%	13%	19%
15–21 days	-	10%	19%	25%	18%	15%	11%	14%	14%
22–28 days	-	-	6%	20%	17%	11%	12%	9%	10%
29–35 days	-	-	-	3%	15%	12%	7%	12%	10%
36–42 days	-	-	-	-	3%	12%	8%	14%	10%
43–49 days	-	-	-	-	-	3%	11%	14%	9%
50–56 days	-	-	-	-	-	-	3%	12%	7%
57–60 days	-	-	-	-	-	-	-	1%	0%
Total	100%	100%	100%	100%	100%	100%	100%	100%	100%
Number	32	42	66	64	65	101	121	562	1,053

Note: Data on six cases were missing from the analysis

Conclusion

Although the overall rate of release onto HDC of eligible prisoners was 30 per cent over the first 16 months of operation, the release rate varied for different types of prisoners and establishments. To a large extent these variations can be explained in terms of variations in reconviction rates across different groups of prisoners. The effect of the risk of reconviction on the decision to release onto HDC can be most clearly seen when comparing reconviction rates of different offence types with the rates of release onto HDC for those offences (HDC release rates decrease for offences with high reconviction rates).

There is no clear link between establishments release and recall rates. This is likely to be a result of differences in inmate populations and in approaches to the HDC assessment process. Variations between Prison Service areas and establishments may also be a result of differences in how HDC has been implemented locally and what Prison Service Area Managers and governors consider to be appropriate levels of risk in deciding whether to release inmates on HDC.

In the first 16 months of operation, the rate of recall was low, with only five per cent of curfewees being recalled to custody by the Prison Service during the period they were subject to HDC.[6] The majority of these recalls were a result of the prisoner breaching his/her curfew conditions. Only eight out of 1,100 prisoners were recalled for posing a risk of serious harm to the public. Recall rates did not vary across different types of prisoner and establishment to the same extent as release rates.

---

6   This only covers prisoners being recalled by the Prison Service. See Chapter 6 for information about reoffending.

4.

Survey of prisoners released on Home Detention Curfew

Introduction

In January 2000, the Home Office commissioned RSGB to undertake research amongst a sample of prisoners released on Home Detention Curfew (HDC). The objectives of the research were to identify the impact of HDC: on curfewees prior to release and on their transition back into the community; on the families of curfewees; and on the work of probation officers supervising curfewees subject to other (non-HDC) licence conditions.

The project included quantitative research among a sample of prisoners released on HDC, as well as sub-samples of their families and supervising Probation Officers. It also included qualitative research among a sample of curfewees who had been recalled to prison. This chapter summarises the key findings from the four strands of the research project: the quantitative curfewee survey; partners/families survey; probation officers survey; and the qualitative research conducted with prisoners recalled to prison.

Methodology

The Home Office provided a sample of all prisoners released onto HDC each week over a five-week period, having first written to give these new curfewees the opportunity to opt out of the research (approximately 5% chose not to take part). From this RSGB drew a stratified random sample of curfewees.[1] A breakdown of the sample group is given in Table 4.9 at the end of this chapter. Using this main curfewee sample, a random sub-sample was selected for interview with a partner or other family member. This family sub-sample was also stratified by the curfewee's sentence length. The Probation Officer sample was drawn at random from a list of all curfewees who had named their Probation Officers and had given their consent for the follow-up interview.

---

[1] This main sample was stratified by sentence length within each HDC region (though an equal sample was drawn for each region, in effect boosting the sample in the Southern region). Random booster samples were also taken of women, ethnic minority prisoners and young offenders.

Curfewees recalled to prison were selected in discussion with the Home Office Research, Development and Statistics Directorate. Given the practical problems of locating prisoners and arranging interviews in very short time-scales, the main factors in selection were to ensure that, wherever possible, two or more recalled curfewees were interviewed on each visit and that all four HDC regions were covered.

Fieldwork was carried out in March, April and May 2000. Face-to-face interviews using Computer Assisted Personal Interviewing (CAPI) were carried out by RSGB field staff with 256 curfewees from an issued sample of 383 (a response rate of 67%). Face-to-face interviews were also conducted in the home using CAPI with family members. Forty-six interviews were achieved from an issued sample of 72 (a response rate of 64%).

Telephone interviews using Computer Assisted Telephone Interviewing (CATI) were conducted with 50 Probation Officers responsible for supervising curfewees who were subject to post-release supervision. Seventeen depth interviews were conducted with recalled curfewees in eight prisons throughout England covering each of the four HDC regions.

The questionnaires for each of three quantitative elements of the study were developed in consultation with the Home Office and Prison Service and were piloted. The qualitative interviews with recalled curfewees used a discussion guide which was also drawn up in consultation with the Home Office and Prison Service.

The data collected from the curfewee survey, other household member survey and Probation Officer survey were weighted at the analysis stage to correct for sampling variation.

Main findings

HDC was viewed positively by the considerable majority of the curfewees, both by those who were still out on their curfew as well as those who had been recalled. It was also viewed positively by members of the curfewees' households and by supervising Probation Officers.

Recalls of curfewees to prison have been steady at the relatively low level of around five to six per cent. This, combined with the positive way in which HDC is viewed, suggests that it has been a successful initiative. However, a number of suggestions for improving the scheme emerged from the surveys.

Areas for improvement

Suggested improvements for the scheme fell under four main headings:

- better preparation and screening of potential curfewees prior to release. This includes clarification of the curfew system, and what curfewees should expect if they violate their curfew
- longer notice time between informing someone that they are going to be released and the release date (though in many cases the time scales for carrying out assessments can make this difficult)
- clarification of support available after release for those who feel that they need to change their curfew address or change the hours of their curfew. Curfewees also need to be told where they can go for advice (e.g. if they are being put under pressure by others, whether intentional or not, to break their curfew)
- the provision of clearer information on HDC to the authorities (police, probation and social services) in the local areas to ensure that they can provide consistent advice.

Overall attitudes towards Home Detention Curfew

When curfewee respondents were first told about HDC, 90 per cent were in favour, with 92 per cent of household members also in favour. At the time of interview, 97 per cent of curfewees said, with the experience of being on HDC, they would still opt for the curfew: only two per cent said they would have preferred to spend the time in prison. Household members were similarly very much in favour of HDC, with only four per cent saying they would have preferred the curfewee to have remained in prison to complete his/her sentence.

Taken as a whole, the probation officers interviewed were also positive about HDC. In relation to a specific named curfewee, 23 per cent said that HDC helped the team's work a lot, while a further 20 per cent felt that it helped their work a little. In general terms (i.e. not related to a specific offender), over three-quarters (76%) of probation officers said that HDC helped their team's work.

Preparation for release

Over a third (37%) of released prisoners interviewed said that the prospect of being released early on HDC affected their behaviour in prison. This was more likely to be mentioned by men (39% versus 17% for women), younger respondents (44% of those aged under 30 versus 29% for those aged 30 plus) and Asian respondents (51% of South Asian,

Chinese and other prisoners, compared with 41% of black and 35% of white respondents).
A fifth (21%) of curfewee respondents said that the opportunity of early release had
encouraged them to take courses or work in prison.

According to Prison Service Order 6700, inmates should receive two weeks' notice
between confirmation of being granted HDC and their release date. In practice, of those
surveyed for this evaluation, barely a third (36%) received this much notice (see Table 4.1).
Of those who received less than two weeks notice, 39 per cent said that this had not been
long enough to prepare themselves.

Table 4.1:   Length of time between confirmation of HDC and release

Length of time	Percentage (base n=256)	Period was long enough	Period was not long enough
Less than one week	39	56	44
1 up to 2 weeks	25	69	31
2 up to 3 weeks	16	90	10
3 up to 4 weeks	11	94	6
4 or more weeks	9	94	6

Provision of information before release

In the interviews with curfewees, respondents were asked what information relating to HDC
had been discussed with them by prison or probation staff before release. The responses
are summarised in Table 4.2. Only seven per cent had actually seen a personal
identification device (PID, or tag) while in prison.

Table 4.2: Information discussed prior to release

Information about HDC	Percentage who had discussed this (base n=256)
Address for the curfew	93
Hours of curfew	82
How the tag should be worn	59
Equipment required in the home	58
Equipment installation process	55
Restrictions other than the hours	49
What the tag looked like	41
Had a tag to look at	7

Eighty-three per cent of curfewees recalled being given something in writing about the curfew rules and 61 per cent said they were given a leaflet about HDC. Less than one in three (29%) had seen the video about HDC. The leaflet appeared to have an impact on the likelihood of breaching curfew: of those who had breached curfew 54 per cent had received a leaflet; this applied to 71 per cent of those who had not broken curfew.

The curfewee sample was evenly split on whether they felt well informed (51%) or poorly informed (49%) prior to release. Those who felt poorly informed were also more likely to report a curfew violation (57% compared with 37%). (Fuller details are in Table 4.3.) This was supported by those who had been recalled. They reported that they were unsure of the rules, how much flexibility, if any, there was in the system and how, if at all, they could change their address or their hours of curfew if they were experiencing problems.

Table 4.3: How well informed were curfewees prior to release

	All respondents (base n=256) %	Curfew violated %	Curfew not violated %
Very well informed	20	48	52
Quite well informed	31	53	47
Quite poorly informed	30	66	34
Very poorly informed	19	78	22

Despite the large proportion who felt at least quite poorly informed about the curfew, relatively few areas were identified where more information was required. The areas mentioned most often were: the nature of the tag and how it would be worn (12%); the monitoring equipment and the effect on the phone line (11%); and how to change the curfew hours (11%).

Perceived advantages and disadvantages of HDC

Prior to release, the main advantages for curfewees of HDC were seen as getting out of prison (82%), freedom (60%), meeting up with family (63%) and getting back home (58%). Details are given in Table 4.4.

Table 4.4:   Perceived advantages (prompted) of HDC for curfewees

Advantages mentioned	Percentage of respondents (base n=256)
Get out of prison	82
Meet up with family	63
Freedom for some hours of the day	60
Get back home	58
Meet up with friends	48
Chance to sort out family/housing/debt problems	38
Start looking for a job/training/education	35
Help to develop some structure/routine to life	35
Earn some money to help out the household/family	32
Get away from other prisoners	29
Prevent mixing with criminal associates	21

Of the 46 interviews with household members, the most commonly cited advantages were having the curfewee home again (72%), an end to the need for prison visits (69%), the curfewee being able to see other family again (50%) and getting the curfewee away from other prisoners (50%). Also mentioned by over a third of household members interviewed were giving the respondent time to do other things (38%), helping the curfewee to develop a structure to his/her life (36%) and sorting out family, housing or debt problems (36%).

Respondents were less likely to mention perceived disadvantages of the curfew. Two-fifths mentioned the restrictions on the time they could spend outside the curfew address, and a quarter mentioned wearing the tag itself (see Table 4.5).

Table 4.5: *Perceived disadvantages (prompted) of HDC for curfewees*

Disadvantages mentioned	Percentage of respondents (base n=256)
Restrictions on the hours out of the home	41
Wearing the tag	27
Problems with finding/keeping a job	23
Inconvenience of curfew hours for other household members	19
Inconvenience of the equipment set-up	12
Increased tensions in relationship with family/friends	10
Having to spend time with family/partner/friends	5

This tallied with the natural reaction of many of those who had been recalled. They reported their delight at being told they were going to be released before later realising that the freedom was only partial. Other household members were also less likely to mention disadvantages than advantages. Those mentioned most often were seeing the curfewee wearing the tag (17%), family and friends finding out about the curfew (15%), having to let the contractors into the home (13%) and the increase in tension in relationships.

HDC and employment

Approximately a third of curfewee respondents were in work – the majority working full-time – at the time of interview. Slightly more were seeking work, and just over a quarter were neither in paid employment, nor seeking work (see Table 4.6).

Table 4.6: *Curfewees and work*

Employment status at time of interview	Percentage of respondents (base n=256)
Full-time paid work	28
Part-time paid work	6
Unemployed, seeking work	36
Not in paid employment, not seeking work	27
In education/retired	3

Curfewees who were in work cited similar advantages and disadvantages of the curfew as other respondents, though they were more likely to mention earning some money (58% compared with 19% of those in other groups) and starting a job (47% versus 29%). They were less likely than others to mention problems with keeping a job because of curfew restrictions (16% compared with 27% for those not in work).

Curfewees who were seeking work were more likely to mention advantages than other groups, particularly developing a routine (44% versus 30%) and looking for a job (60% compared with 21%). This group was also more likely to mention disadvantages than other groups, such as the problem of finding or keeping a job (33% compared with 18% of those in other groups) and the inconvenience of the curfew hours on other household members (24% versus 16%).

While over a third of curfewee respondents were working at the time of interview, findings from the interviews with those recalled to prison suggested that there could be a conflict between their employment and the curfew restrictions. In particular, the need to work shifts, long hours, or to do overtime, often at short notice, created problems for some who had been working and, in some cases, directly to the breach and the subsequent recall to custody.

Family relationships under curfew

While 67 per cent of curfewees said that the curfew had made no difference to their relationship with others, 22 per cent said that relationships had improved. Ten per cent said that relationships had got worse and seven per cent reported problems in relationships with others in the household that they put down to the curfew.

Similarly in 69 per cent of cases the other household member interviewed said that the curfew period had made no difference to their relationship with the curfewee. In 25 per cent of cases they said that it had made the relationship better, while four per cent said that it had made the relationship worse.

Among the household members interviewed, a higher percentage said that the curfew was beneficial in terms of giving them time to do other things (35%) than felt that the curfew adversely affected the time they had to do what they wanted (18%). The main time benefits related to having more social time with family or friends, more time to spend by themselves or more time to spend with their children. The evidence suggests that, on balance, the curfew had a neutral or slightly positive effect on relationships.

Contact with the electronic monitoring staff

In general, the staff of the electronic monitoring contractors were rated very highly by curfewees. Ninety-eight per cent said that they were very or fairly polite, 95 per cent that they were very or fairly helpful, and 95 per cent that they were very or fairly professional. Only 12 per cent felt that the contractors were fairly, or very, intrusive. In 95 per cent of cases, curfewees reported that the contractors had explained how the equipment worked, and in 97 per cent of these cases, the curfewee said that the information was sufficient.

Curfew violations

Three-fifths (61%) of respondents reported that they had experienced a curfew violation (see Table 4.7).[2] The majority of these (63%) were reported by the curfewee to be the result of equipment malfunction (though neither the electronic monitoring contractors nor the Home Office became aware of any significant equipment problems).

Table 4.7: **Claimed reasons for curfew violation**

Violation reason	Percentage of respondents (base n=256)
No violation	39
Equipment failure	38
Delayed by transport breakdown/delays	7
Stepped out of range	6
Stayed out too late with family/friends	4
Any non-equipment reason	22

Fifty per cent of the 155 respondents who reported having had a curfew violation received a visit from the contractor specifically to check the equipment and two-fifths (39 per cent) received a telephone call from the contractor. Eleven per cent received a visit from the contractor to ask about the violation, and nine per cent received a warning letter.[3] One in seven (14%) said that nothing had happened as a result of the claimed violation.

---

2   "Curfew violation" means that the curfewee broke the rules of the curfew. The question was worded so as to ask curfewees if they had experienced a violation, regardless of whether they felt that they had actually infringed the rules. In addition to cases where there was an acknowledged breaking of the curfew rules, responses would therefore also pick up cases where the curfewee felt that there had been no violation but s/he was contacted by the monitoring companies in relation to an alleged violation.

3   Respondents could report more than one outcome, and there could have been different outcomes in cases where a curfewee reported more than one violation. Hence the percentages total more than 100.

Contact with probation staff

Curfewees were asked about meetings they had had with the probation service. Three-quarters (74% of all respondents) had met with a probation officer since their release. This applied to all but one of those with a sentence of one year or more (99%) and all but one of those released from a Young Offender Institution (93%).

Although there was a sense of compulsion in meetings with the probation service, in the majority of cases (67%) these were thought to be "generally helpful" (28% reported the meetings as being "generally unhelpful"). The majority (70%) felt that they had about the right level of help from the probation service. Twelve per cent said they would have liked help from the probation service to find suitable accommodation.

Taken as a group, the probation officers interviewed were also positive about HDC. *In relation to a specific named curfewee*, 23 per cent said that HDC helped the team's work a lot and another 20 per cent felt that it helped their work a little. Six per cent said that it hindered their work a little. (The biggest response, from 53% of probation officer respondents, felt that HDC made no difference to the work of the team.) In relation to a named offender, the main benefits reported were that HDC gave the curfewee a routine to work within (18%) and that it gave the curfewee a more positive outlook(17%). Fourteen per cent of probation officers also mentioned that HDC gave them a strong bargaining tool with the offender.

In general terms (i.e. not related to a specific offender), over three-quarters (76%) of probation officers said that HDC helped their team's work. The profile of answers was similar to that for specific named offenders: 43 per cent said that HDC gave curfewees more of a routine; 23 per cent said that it made curfewees less likely to break other restrictions; 17 per cent said that it gave offenders a more positive outlook; and one in seven (14%) felt it would make curfewees more likely to stay away from trouble.

Negative comments by probation officers about HDC in general included that it made interview times more awkward (12%), especially for working curfewees, it was associated with increased paperwork (10%) and that it could make it harder to gain the support of employers/training providers (9%).

Recalled curfewees

Depth interviews were carried out in prison with 17 curfewees who had been recalled to custody following a breakdown in their curfew. (The recall rate nationally has been stable and running at around five per cent for most of the time since the scheme was introduced.) The aim of these interviews was to find out what lay behind the breach of the curfew. The factors underlying the recall to prison fell into four main categories: equipment; psychological; housing/domestic; and lifestyle (see Table 4.8).[4]

Table 4.8:   Factors underlying breach of HDC for recalled curfewees

Equipment	Psychological	Housing/domestic	Lifestyle
Equipment problems (alleged)	Motivation	Housing problems	Work
	Addictions	Family support	Hedonism
	Recidivism	Social environment	Drugs/alcohol
	Anger management		

Equipment issues
Claimed equipment problems could lead curfewees into potential conflict with monitoring staff, who have a duty to investigate alleged violations. In the case of at least one recalled curfewee interviewed for this project, the visit by monitoring staff made him so angry that he became abusive and threatening towards them. This then led directly to his recall.

Psychological issues
Motivation was a key issue, with a number of those interviewed appearing to have been unable to exert enough self-discipline to keep to the curfew. Some had experienced problems with returning to drug or alcohol use, or to the life of crime that they had known prior to prison. There were also problems for some with anger management, and arguments with other members of the household or with the monitoring staff that could lead (directly or indirectly) to recall.

Housing and domestic issues
Problems with unsuitable housing or unstable tenure were a factor in some of those interviewed being recalled to prison. Relationship problems were often associated with either a loss of accommodation or curfew violations. Family support was also an important factor in a curfewee's ability to cope on HDC. Isolation and boredom were particular problems for those living by themselves.

---

4   These factors were frequently overlapping.

Lifestyle issues

The need to be available to work shifts, long hours or to do overtime, especially at short notice, can conflict with the curfew requirements. This can also make it harder for some curfewees to find or take work. On the other hand, some of the recalled prisoners interviewed were characterised by a hedonistic lifestyle and once released went back to the largely nocturnal activities of pubs and clubs, disregarding the requirements of the curfew. The impact of drug and alcohol use on the ability to keep to curfew times or other licence conditions was also a significant factor in some recalls.

Post-release support

An area in which curfewees were asking for improvement was support after release. The contractors received high ratings from respondents in the quantitative research and were praised in the qualitative research also. However, beyond this, many of the breaches in curfew were related to inability to get help or a lack of knowledge of who to turn to.

Those who had problems with housing (such as drug users – or former users – who found themselves in "using" households) reported that attempts to get help with relocation were fruitless. Some curfewees had contacted police or probation officers on experiencing problems with the curfew, only to find that they knew little or nothing about the scheme. Some curfewees also reported that they were reluctant to contact the contractors directly in the fear that they would be recalled instantly.

This again emphasises that, prior to release, curfewees need to be given material that explains the type of help they can expect to receive on release. It also suggests that the local bodies (police, probation and social services) need to be better briefed on HDC, what flexibility, if any, exists in the system and who should take responsibility for support after release. This would require more local networking in connection with HDC than appears to be taking place at present.

Qualities needed for a successful curfew

On the basis of the samples making up this survey, a number of elements appear to contribute to the smooth and successful passing of the HDC period. Among these are the following:

- realism
- self-discipline (e.g. managing time, fighting addictions, avoiding previous criminal associates and lifestyle)
- support from others after release (personal and professional)
- forward planning (e.g. knowing what pressures they will face, adequate time to plan and prepare)
- a stable and suitable environment to live in (probation checks on suitability can be very important in ensuring this)
- a clear understanding of the rules (for curfewees *and* other household members, family and friends).

Can prisoners be better prepared for release on HDC?

Most of the recalled curfewees interviewed said that the lure of "freedom" on HDC was very strong and made it less likely that those being assessed would be realistic about the chances of their completing the curfew period. This, coupled with the high numbers who felt poorly informed, suggests that more could be done to inform and prepare prisoners both before and during the assessment process so that they understand some of the pressures that they will face and have a chance to think about how to cope with them.

Some of the breaches, notably among those who were motivated to complete their curfew, appeared to be the result of a lack of communication or even miscommunication. There was confusion as to whether, and in what circumstances, a warning rather than recall would be used. This meant that some curfewees believed that one episode of lateness would result in a warning while others believed that it would result in recall to prison.

Concerns in connection with the quality and consistency of information appeared to be common across all types of curfewee, including those motivated to succeed. This suggests that there may be a need for an improved pre-release information package.

The research found that excitement prior to release was not conducive to people being receptive to information. Some possible suggestions for making this process more effective were:

- to ensure that prisoners are informed of the key restrictions under the curfew and any practices which are inappropriate for the monitoring equipment (this could be included if the video shown to prisoners is updated)
- give prisoners testimonials from a range of other curfewees to enable the new curfewee to understand the type of pressures they are going to be faced with and the coping strategies that others have found successful (this could also be included in a revised video)
- give prisoners clear guidance on what can be done if they are finding it difficult to cope with the curfew and need to change hours, change address or seek other forms of support
- to provide a leaflet for reference after starting the curfew which re-states the key points from the video and gives clear guidance on the support that is available at the local level
- wherever possible, allow at least two weeks between notifying the prisoner that s/he has been granted HDC and the date of starting HDC. This gives the prisoner time to make mental and practical preparations for release and gives prison staff more time to ensure that prisoners are properly informed and prepared prior to release.

Who is suitable for HDC?

Recalled curfewees were consistent in their views of the type of people they thought were suitable for HDC: those people with family or friends they could call upon for support and those people placed in an environment away from their "old life". This would take them out of their circle of contacts where they were likely to encounter drugs or the temptations of alcohol or those who would encourage them back to crime. It would give them the chance to start afresh and develop a new structure to their lives.

It was generally thought that HDC was better for those with jobs as they had something that could relieve the monotony of the curfew. However, it was also recognised that the presence of a job put additional strain on the curfew period – curfewees had to leave work in sufficient time to return home allowing for transport problems. Respondents were also usually unwilling to let work colleagues know that they were on HDC and this too created stress.

It was widely thought that those who were drug or alcohol dependent would find it very difficult to survive on curfew. One recalled curfewee for example, reported that s/he went back on to drugs because of the boredom of the curfew hours.

While, with hindsight, recognising the stresses of the curfew period, curfewees reported that it was considered weak if they did not accept the curfew. Great emphasis was placed by other inmates on "getting out" and little on the fact that HDC is a stepping stone. This suggests that HDC may need to be presented differently within prisons so that prospective curfewees see it as something which can help their re-integration, rather than as an end in itself.

Conclusion

HDC is viewed positively by curfewees, their families and supervising probation officers. This is reflected in the findings that just two per cent of the curfewees interviewed said that they would rather have stayed in prison than be released on curfew and that only four per cent of household members said that they wished the curfewee had remained in prison.

Completion rates for HDC have remained high, and there is some evidence that it may be helping to improve the transition to the community for at least some curfewees. With better preparation of prisoners before release, clearer understanding of the rules by curfewees and families, improved information about post-release support for curfewees and more awareness of the HDC scheme among local agencies with which the curfewee may come into contact, better re-integration of prisoners into the community may be achieved.

Sample structure

The sample of curfewees was structured to reflect the eligible HDC population on the basis of region, sentence length, gender, age, ethnicity and type of establishment. The breakdown of the sample is shown in Table 4.9.

Table 4.9: Structure of main curfewee sample

	Unweighted (n=256) Percentage	Weighted (n=256) Percentage
Sex		
Men	82	91
Women	18	9
Age		
18–20	8	8
21–24	25	23
25–29	20	20
30–39	28	29
40–49	12	12
50+	8	9
Ethnicity		
White	74	84
Black – Caribbean, African, other	10	8
South Asian, Chinese and other	16	7
HDC region		
London & Eastern	25	23
Northern	28	31
Southern	20	16
Midlands & Wales	28	30
Sentence length		
3 months + but less than 1 year	40	50
12 months + but less than 4 years	60	50
Type of establishment		
Young Offender Institution	19	17
Open prison	32	31
Closed/training prison	24	20
Local prison	25	31

5. Cost-benefit analysis of Home Detention Curfew

Introduction

The evaluation plan for the HDC scheme prior to its introduction in January 1999 included a commitment to re-visit the cost-benefit analysis carried out in the original appraisal work. The following chapter attempts to quantify and value all of the costs and benefits of HDC. These are calculated, where possible, in terms of the resources used, and are not necessarily equal to cash payments made or received. The results are compared with the cost benefit analysis that was carried out during the development of the scheme. The report also identifies the key factors affecting the costs and benefits, and considers what might happen in the future.

The main *costs* of the scheme can be separated into three stages. The first is the pre-release risk assessment carried out in prisons and probation services. After release the Home Office makes payments to contractors to monitor the curfews. Finally, for a small number of offenders, there is the cost of recall following a breach of HDC licence conditions.

In terms of the *benefits* of the scheme, HDC was designed to provide a 'managed transition between custody and living in the community… and also provide some structure and order into often disorganised lives'.[1] The scheme has also had the effect of reducing the demand for prison places.

This chapter focuses on the costs and benefits of the first year of the scheme. However it has been possible to update the overall analysis to take account of the first 16 months. The overall findings for both the first 12 and first 16 months are shown in Table 5.1.

---

1 Statement made by Home Secretary Jack Straw on 28 January 1999 in response to a Parliamentary Question from Lorna Fitzsimons, MP for Rochdale.

Table 5.1: Summary of costs and benefits of Home Detention Curfew

Agency	12 Months		16 Months	
	Estimated Cost	Benefit	Estimated Cost	Benefit
Prison staff costs	£3.2m		£4.3m	
Probation services	£2.3m		£3.0m	
Contractor costs (actual charges made ex. VAT)	£21.0m		£27.9m	
Sentence Enforcement Unit	£0.15m		£0.2m	
Prison resource savings		£63.4m		£84.6m
Net benefits	£36.7m^2		£49.2m^2	
Prison places saved	1950		2600	

The total cost of the first year of operation was slightly under £26.7 million, rising to £35.4 million for the first 16 months. This has reduced demand for prison places by around 1,950 places in the first year (2,600 in the first 16 months).[3] By far the largest cost was charges made by the contractors monitoring offenders.

Translating the number of prison places 'saved' into a resource saving (£63.4m for the first 12 months of the scheme) makes it possible to show that the net benefit (benefits minus costs) in monetary terms was £36.7m in the first year. This does not represent a reduction in Prison Service cash flows, since many of the prison places freed may be used to reduce overcrowding[4] or house different prisoners.[5]

---

2 Not including start-up costs, except for the monitoring contractors.
3 The figure of 1,950 places is slightly lower than previously published figures because it includes start-up period in the first two months of the scheme. The equivalent figure for the first 12 months when the scheme was fully operational was 1,960.
4 Around 12,000 prisoners were held two to a cell designed for one in 1999/2000.
5 The short run 'cashable' saving resulting from removing a single prisoner from prison is relatively small, since prisons must still be maintained and staff levels are unlikely to change. However in the long run there may be other resource savings, for example there is a reduced need to build new prisons, which may reduce expenditure required on capital for the Prison Service.

Prison Service

Prior to the launch of HDC, the Prison Service carried out a simple costing exercise to investigate the likely cost of implementing the HDC risk assessment process in prisons. At the time they estimated the cost to be £4.1 million for the first year of operation.

As a part of the evaluation process the actual costs of the process following the introduction of the scheme were investigated. This type of information is not routinely recorded, so a simple activity sampling exercise was carried out. This involved a sample of eight prisons,[6] where every member of staff involved in HDC was asked to record the amount of time they spent on various stages of the process over a two-week period. This made it possible to calculate the total staff costs of HDC to the Prison Service. It also allowed comparison between prisons to see what the important factors controlling costs were.

The activity sampling exercise captured all elements of the risk assessment process, from the issuing of the 'HDC2' form which confirms an offender's wish to participate, through to release, and then post-release activities. The average time taken to complete the whole process was around 4 hours 15 minutes per HDC2 form issued,[7] and cost around £60. Based on this estimate, the total cost of HDC to the Prison Service was around £3.2 million in the first year.[8]

A comparison between prisons was carried out to investigate whether particular types of prison, or categories of prisoner might have an impact on the cost of the process. The analysis indicates that there is little evidence of this type of correlation. There is a weak relationship between the cost of completing the HDC1 risk assessment form and the size of the prison. This suggests there may be some economies of scale to the process, however the link is relatively tenuous.

---

6   Ten prisons were included in the exercise but only eight returned sufficient information to include them in the analysis.

7   The activity sampling exercise took place over a two-week period, however a risk assessment in a prison may take up to ten weeks to be completed. For this reason the analysis assumes that there is an approximately constant flow of offenders through the process, and the proportions at each stage remain constant. This would imply that the cost per HDC2 form would also remain constant. In practice however one prison had an exceptionally large number of offenders who became eligible for HDC in the second week of the exercise. Much of the work for this influx was carried out in the following weeks, and so was not captured by the exercise. This means that for this prison the cost per HDC2 form was an under estimate, and for this reason it has been excluded from this analysis.

8   This is calculated assuming all prisoners defined as eligible for HDC will receive an HDC2 form. There may be some under-recording of assessments, however there is no evidence to suggest that eligible prisoners are not being assessed for release on HDC.

Figure 5.1 below shows the average cost of completing each of the major stages of Home Detention Curfew for all of the prisons in the sample. The cost of appealing against a decision not to release, requesting a variation in curfew conditions, and the cost of recalled prisoners are all based on extremely small samples, and should be treated with caution.[9]

Figure 5.1 Cost of completing each stage of the HDC process, per completion [10]

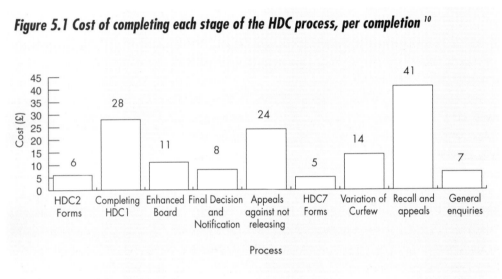

All values are rounded to the nearest £

The main cost is the number of risk assessments carried out. This stage includes issuing HDC2 forms, completing the HDC1 risk assessment form, the enhanced board and making the final decision, and represents around 65 per cent of the total cost of HDC to the Prison Service. This cost is incurred whether the prisoner is released or not.[11]

The number of risk assessments will drive most of the cost of HDC to the Prison Service rather than the number actually released. The number of assessments is dependent on the number of prisoners eligible for HDC. Prison population forecasts suggest that the number of prisoners will increase over the next few years. Provided the proportion of the population eligible remains constant, this growth would suggest the workload for the Prison Service will rise. However, offenders who breach HDC once will no longer be eligible for HDC if they are reconvicted and sent to custody at a later date. This may reduce the proportion of the prison population eligible for HDC.

---

9   For example it is not clear whether the cost of recall and appeal is as high as the sample suggests, or whether there was one, particularly difficult case, which may have biased the results.

10 Note that the cost of enquiries is per HDC2 form issued, since the number of enquiries is not known.

11 Although some prisoners may drop out of the risk assessment after completing the HDC2 form if they choose not to be considered for HDC.

Probation services

Probation services are involved in completing part of the risk assessment for offenders who are being considered for release on HDC. They consider factors such as the suitability of the curfew address proposed by the offender, and the likely impact on any victims. In most cases the local probation service will undertake a home visit to view the curfew address and to talk to residents at this address, although in some cases where the family is known to the service, a telephone call is often used.

There was no direct activity sampling analysis looking at the cost of HDC to probation services in this first year, however there is some evidence from various local services of the time taken to complete a risk assessment. These estimates range from around two hours (as suggested by ACOP) to 4 hours 15 minutes,[12] to complete a probation risk assessment. The cost partly depends on the grade of staff involved. We might expect there to be trade off between the grade and the time taken, with lower grades taking longer to complete the task.

It has been assumed that the average time taken to complete an assessment is 3 hours 15 minutes (the mean of the estimates available). In addition it is assumed that half of the staff time involved in completing a probation risk assessment will involve a Probation Service Officer grade, and the other half a Probation Officer grade. Given these assumptions it is possible to estimate that each risk assessment costs around £60 (including an allowance for travelling and accommodation costs such as renting office space).

The prison activity sampling exercise mentioned previously has allowed us to estimate the number of probation risk assessments requested by the Prison Service. Approximately half of all offenders eligible for HDC had the probation assessment, which implies that slightly under 27,000[13] offenders were assessed in the first year. Given the cost, and the estimated number of assessments, the total cost of the risk assessment process to Probation Services was around £1.6 million in the first year.[14] This may be an underestimate since an evaluation carried out in 1999 noted that initially the majority of offenders received a probation assessment. As the year has progressed the sifting process has improved, reducing the number of assessments required. The prison activity sampling exercise (carried out in March 2000) will not capture this decline.

---

12 Although the probation service that produced the higher estimates also stated that they had some spare capacity, which may mean this time was an overestimate.

13 Note that ACOP suggested that this figure may be slightly lower at around 23,400 for the first year. However this was based on data from one probation service, whereas the activity sampling exercise selected a national sample.

14 This excludes the cost of assessing requests by offenders to change address.

Probation services must also include an assessment of HDC in some pre-sentence reports, where HDC is a possibility for offenders who may be sentenced to custody. This results in increased workload for Probation officers. ACOP have estimated that this may add approximately 15 minutes to around half of all pre-sentence reports written. This would add slightly over £0.6 million to the cost of the HDC scheme, giving a total cost of £2.3 million.[15]

The cost of HDC to probation services was not included in the initial cost benefit report, although was included in later modelling.

The number of assessments completed is the main cost driver in the case of Probation Services. It was previously mentioned that an increasing prison population may lead to an increase in the number of prison assessments carried out, which is likely to affect the number of probation assessments completed. On the other hand, the more effective prisons are at sifting out prisoners who are unlikely to pass the whole risk assessment, the fewer assessments need to go to Probation Services.

Contractor costs

The three contractors, GSSC, Premier Monitoring Services and Securicor Custodial Services, charged the Home Office a total of £21 million excluding VAT for running the HDC scheme between 28 January 1999 and 31 January 2000. This was the cost of monitoring the 16,000 offenders released on curfew in the first year of the scheme.

The initial cost-benefit analysis carried out in 1997 (before the submission of bids for the contracts) estimated that contractor charges would be around £19.7 million, based on 30,000 offenders being released. Hence the actual cost of monitoring was £1.3 million higher than originally predicted, despite a little over half the expected number of offenders being released on the scheme.

The average cost per offender released is higher than was expected in 1997, at around £1,300 per curfew, compared to about £700 that had originally been estimated. There had been no negotiations with the various contractors in 1997 and the estimated cost of monitoring was based on information from the trials of curfew orders, which had been running since July 1995. A model of the contractor costs was developed as a part of the evaluation process of the second year of curfew order trials.[16] This model was used to forecast the likely cost of monitoring Home Detention Curfew.

---

15 Discrepancy due to rounding.
16 See Mortimer & May, 1997.

In practice the contractor charges *per curfewee* for HDC are significantly higher per curfewee at low demand levels, than those for curfew orders. As actual release rates on HDC are lower than originally anticipated, this may explain why the initial estimates of the average cost were significantly below the actual costs.

The volume of offenders released on tag directly determines the charges made by contractors to the Home Office. Anything that changes the risk profile of the prison population, the assessment of risks by prison governors, or legislation that adjusts the release rates for prisons will by definition change the cost to the Home Office of contractor payments. However if demand remains at its current level, contractor charges will fall in real terms, since the contracts contain an RPI-X clause.[17]

Sentence Enforcement Unit

The Sentence Enforcement Unit (SEU – formerly Parole Unit) at Prison Service HQ dedicated resources worth around £175,000 during the first year of HDC to the recall of offenders in breach of the HDC licence condition, or who had committed a further offence. This has been scaled down to reflect the fact that the Unit could have handled an estimated 15 per cent more cases in the first year (as the number of recalls was lower than had been anticipated). Therefore, the actual estimated cost of HDC to SEU was likely to be slightly under £150,000 for the first year of the scheme, including the cost of travel and subsistence payments and accommodation costs (estimated to be 20% of staff costs).

Offenders whose original offence was committed after 1 January 1999 who commit a further offence whilst on HDC can be recalled by SEU (in consultation with the Parole Board) using Section 39 of the Crime and Disorder Act. Offenders sentenced before 1 January 1999 who reoffend whilst on curfew cannot be recalled by SEU unless they have also breached their HDC licence conditions. For this group of offenders, the reoffending falls to the courts to deal with as a breach. Over time the number of offenders on HDC sentenced before this date will fall, and so the number of offenders recalled using Section 39 is likely to rise. The expectation is that the overall recall rate will remain constant.

The process of recalling offenders using Section 39 is estimated to take around one and a half times longer than a recall for breach of HDC licence conditions as it involves liaison with the Parole Board. So the cost of HDC to SEU is expected to rise slightly in the future, reflecting the increased number of recalls carried out in this way.

---

17 The contractor charges will change by the rate of inflation (the RPI), minus some factor (X), which is defined in the contracts. This means charges will increase at less than the rate of inflation so the real cost will fall over the period of the contracts, which expire in 2004.

The estimated cost of the Unit compares to an original estimate of around £60,000 a year in the cost-benefit analysis, despite around half the number of offenders expected being recalled. The main reason for the higher cost of recalling offenders who breach HDC is due to a higher unit cost, at almost £100[18] per recall compared to the £40 originally estimated. This difference has offset the lower than anticipated number of recalls.

Other costs

There were a number of other costs identified in the original cost benefit analysis. These were:

- the cost to the police of dealing with recalled offenders was included in the initial appraisal. However this cost is likely to be small due to the small number of recalls that occurred in the first year, and has been excluded from this analysis
- there were a number of one-off start up costs for the Prison Service, probation services and the Sentence Enforcement Unit. These were estimated at around £1.5 million in the original cost-benefit analysis. However this evaluation considers only the ongoing costs of the scheme, and so the net benefit estimates do not include these start up costs.

Benefits of HDC

It was anticipated that the main quantifiable benefit of the HDC scheme would be to reduce the prison population, resulting in some long term resource savings for the Prison Service. Offenders released on curfew reduce the prison population and so free up prison places. When the scheme was first considered it was expected that this would contribute to reducing the overcrowding of prisons that was anticipated in the late 1990s.[19]

The HDC scheme freed up an estimated 1,950 prison places in its first year of operation. This means that the scheme has reduced the extent to which new prisons are needed to meet forecasts of the prison population into the first decade of the new millennium.

These prison places represent a resource saving to the Prison Service. Based on the mix of prisons involved in releasing offenders on HDC it is possible to estimate that the scheme has saved around £63.4 million. As mentioned previously this is a long run resource saving and not a short run reduction in the annual expenditure of the Prison Service. The short-term

---

18 This figure does not take into account overhead costs of policy and management tasks.

19 The Prison Service Annual Report and Accounts, April 1999 to March 2000, quoted an overcrowding rate of 18.9 per cent (p.11). This is "the number of priosners held two to a cell designed for one, expressed as a percentage of the average [prison] population".

benefits of a reduced prison population are relatively small, since prisons must be staffed to their operational capacity, not their current population. However in the longer term there is a reduced need to invest in increasing the prison capacity, and it is this long run resource saving that is estimated in the cost-benefit evaluation.

The original cost-benefit analysis estimated that the scheme would save around 3,700 prison places in the first year of operation. If a similar resource cost saving had been attached, then the expected benefit would have been around £111 million.[20] This is significantly higher than the actual saving because the release rate has been lower than originally expected.

Conclusion

The HDC scheme, in terms of its cost and benefits, appears to have been a relative success. In the first year of operation the scheme has resulted in a net benefit of around £36.7 million (excluding non-contractor start up costs of £1.5 million). This trend has continued into the second year, with the net benefit for the first 16 months being £49.2 million.

The costs of the scheme, overall, have been slightly higher than anticipated. In particular payments to contractors were higher than originally anticipated. However the cost of the risk assessment process in prisons is lower than the £4.1m originally estimated.

The net saving might be expected to increase in the future, as the cost of payments to contractors for monitoring offenders will fall in real terms. At the same time the prison population is forecast to increase over the next few years implying that the eligible population (and total net benefits of the scheme) will increase.

---

20 In practice the original appraisal handled these in a slightly different way since it assumed that overcrowding would occur in the absence of HDC, and relatively expensive police cells would be used.

6.   Reconvictions of offenders released
                             on Home Detention Curfew

This chapter examines the relationship between Home Detention Curfew and recidivism. The level of reoffending, leading to reconviction, during and after the HDC period is presented and comparisons are made with a control group of offenders discharged from custody in autumn 1998. The rate of offending after completion of HDC was very close to that of the control group for similar lengths of time following discharge from prison. Comparison of the results of risk prediction tools with patterns of release rates suggests that approval for release on HDC was closely but not solely dependent on the predicted probability of reoffending. The minority of offenders with a high predicted probability who were nevertheless granted HDC experienced lower than predicted levels of reoffending, suggesting that the risk assessment process had been effective in taking account of their personal circumstances.

Methodology

To evaluate the impact of HDC on reoffending, the Police National Computer (PNC) records of offenders eligible for HDC in certain months were analysed to detect reoffending during and after the curfew period. These offenders (known as the programme group) were compared with a control group of those released prior to the launch of the scheme who would have been eligible for HDC had it been available. Given that the control group contains offenders who would not have been granted HDC, and that it is not possible to tell which offenders would have been granted or refused, the programme group must also include offenders not granted HDC. Offenders in the programme group were eligible for release on HDC (if granted) in May and June 1999, while the control group were discharged in September and October 1998.

The reoffending (leading to reconviction: this should be taken to be the case throughout this chapter) of offenders granted HDC was measured during the curfew period. Also, the reoffending of all offenders in the study was measured separately for a certain period from the date of discharge *on which they would have been discharged had they been refused HDC.*[1] The 'six-month' follow-up of an offender eligible for HDC on 1 June 1999 and for

---

1   Depending on the sentence length, this is either the Conditional Release Date or Automatic Release Date.

automatic discharge on 1 July 1999 would therefore cover reoffending between 1 July 1999 and 1 January 2000 whether or not the offender was granted HDC. This methodology allows clear comparison between the control and programme groups.[2]

Further methodological details are presented in the 'Technical notes' section at the end of this chapter.

Offending while on curfew

The occurrence of reoffending specifically during the curfew period, measured on the basis described in the 'Technical notes', is presented in Table 6.1.

Table 6.1:   *Reconviction rate for offences committed while subject to HDC*

Reconvicted	31
	2.1%
Not reconvicted	1,464
	97.9%
Total	1,495
	100%

The rate of reoffending is shown to be close to two per cent. This is slightly lower than the rate for the whole of 1999 presented in answers to Parliamentary Questions in May 2000[3] (2.4%), but this rate included cautions and impending prosecutions outstanding at the time, as well as convictions secured more than six months after the offence took place.[4]

---

2   There is a concern that this disregards the reduction in the incapacitative effect of imprisonment caused by those granted HDC being released earlier than their counterparts in the control group. In practice, however, the effect is fairly small – counting from the HDC release date would raise the reoffending rates for the "granted HDC" offenders in Table 6.2 by about 1 percentage point, causing a rise of about one-third of a percentage point in the rates for the whole of the programme group.

3   Written question no. 123374 from Phil Hope MP (Corby), 22 May 2000. Weekly Hansard (Commons) issue 1863, column 360W.

4   Additionally, a rate of 2.7 per cent was obtained for those granted HDC in February 1999. Data for February were analysed but are not presented as difficulties associated with the launch of the scheme make this an unrepresentative month.

Offending after the curfew period

Table 6.2 below presents reoffending rates, measured on the basis described above (under 'Methodology'). After removing incomplete records, and using prison discharge files to supplement HDC-specific records, the number of satisfactory follow-ups of offenders granted and not granted curfew did not perfectly reflect the known relative proportions of these offenders. A weighting procedure was therefore applied. The rates for the whole programme group are calculated as a weighted average of those for offenders granted and not granted curfew[5] to ensure that the rates for the whole programme group reflect the real proportion granted HDC rather than merely the proportion among those who could be satisfactorily traced in the computer records.

The rates are cumulative, so, for example, the three-month rate includes offences committed during the first, second and third months following the automatic discharge date.

---

5   In May and June 1999 combined, 32 per cent of those eligible were granted HDC, so the reoffending rate for the whole programme group is calculated as 0.32*"granted HDC" rate + 0.68*"not granted HDC" rate.

Table 6.2: *Reconviction rates for offences committed up to six months after normal discharge date (not including offences during the HDC period) for those granted HDC, not granted HDC and a control group*

| Follow-up period | Percentage reconvicted (number eligible for follow-up to this point)[6] | | | |
	Programme group: granted HDC	Programme group: not granted HDC	Whole programme group (weighted)	Control group
1 month	2.0	10.2	7.6	7.6
	(1493)	(5292)	(6785)	(6,888)
2 months	4.5	18.4	14.0	14.1
	(1491)	(5237)	(6728)	(6,857)
3 months	6.5	25.4	19.3	19.0
	(1488)	(5185)	(6673)	(6,828)
4 months	8.3	31.4	24.0	23.2
	(1288)	(4549)	(5837)	(6,797)
5 months	10.0	37.4	28.6	26.9
	(627)	(2552)	(3179)	(6,759)
6 months	9.3	40.5	30.5	30.0
	(118)	(558)	(676)	(6,723)

These rates show that those granted HDC have far lower reconviction rates than those who are refused it – typically the former group's rate is about one-quarter of that of the latter group. The weighted average of the pilot group members is always very close to that of the control group. The differences between the programme group and the control group are not statistically significant.

---

6   Offenders can be excluded from a follow-up because they were not discharged early enough for the follow-up to be completed by the point at which data was collected from the Police National Computer, or because a pseudoreconviction (i.e. for an offence which preceded the original prison sentence) which results in imprisonment disrupts the follow-up period. In either case, an offender may be included in shorter follow-up periods but excluded from longer ones. The five-month reconviction for the programme group is actually higher than for the six-month follow-up. This provides an explanation for the programme group having a higher reconviction rate after five months than six – it is partly a result of the much smaller number of cases that it was possible to follow up for the longer period. Fuller details of the follow-up timetable and an explanation of pseudoreconvictions are included in the 'Technical notes' section at the end of this chapter. The 'numbers eligible' presented for the whole programme group do not take account of the weighting procedure.

If offences committed during the HDC period (which resulted in conviction) are taken into account, the reconviction rates for offenders granted HDC rise by an average of around one percentage point and the figures for the whole programme group rise by 0.3 to 0.4 of a percentage point.[7]

Risk assessment and the decision to grant HDC

In order to model the risk of reoffending within four months, the longest period for which most offenders could be tracked, Offender Group Reconviction Scale (OGRS) scores for each offender were generated using Police National Computer (PNC) data and mathematically transformed to reflect the shorter follow-up period.[8] Average levels of risk of detected reoffending were virtually identical for the programme and control groups, at 23.6 and 23.5 per cent respectively. Table 6.3 examines in more detail levels of predicted risk for the programme group.

Table 6.3:   Predicted risk of reoffending and assessment outcome[9]

Predicted risk of reoffending within 4 months of discharge or end of curfew period	Percentage of all programme group offenders	Percentage granted HDC
Up to 10%	34.6	58
11 to 20%	16.0	34
21 to 30%	11.9	24
31 to 40%	13.0	15
41 to 50%	13.0	8
51 to 60%	10.9	5
Over 60%	0.6	0
All offenders (n=12,627)	100	32

7   On this basis, the follow-up reconviction figures for offenders granted HDC are: 1 month – 3.4 per cent; 2 months – 5.8 per cent; 3 months – 7.7 per cent; 4 months – 9.4 per cent; 5 months – 10.5 per cent; and 6 months – 10.2 per cent. For the programme group as a whole, the figures are: 1 month – 8.0 per cent; 2 months –14.4 per cent; 3 months – 19.7 per cent; 4 months – 24.3 per cent; 5 months – 28.8 per cent; and 6 months – 30.8 per cent. Figures for those not granted HDC and for the control group are not affected.

8   As only 31 programme group members reoffended during the curfew period, an analysis of the factors associated with reoffending during this period is impractical within the design of this study.

9   All percentages have been weighted so that they reflect the actual percentage of offenders granted and not granted HDC, rather than the percentage among those studied. All percentages refer only to those who could be followed up for four months.

This confirms that low-risk offenders are more likely to be granted curfew and that the chance of curfew continues to decline as risk rises. Offenders with a risk of short-term reoffending below 10 per cent were twice as likely as average to be curfewed, while those with a risk above 40 per cent were exceptionally unlikely to be granted HDC.

Table 6.4 examines the reoffending outcome for those who were granted curfew and gives more detail of the predicted risk levels of these offenders.

Table 6.4: **Predicted and actual rates of reoffending among those granted Home Detention Curfew**

Predicted risk of reoffending within 4 months of discharge or end of curfew period	Number of offenders granted HDC	Percentage of those granted HDC	Percentage reoffending	Percentage predicted to reoffend
Up to 10%	815	63.4	2	5
11 to 20%	217	16.9	16	14
21 to 30%	114	8.9	19	25
31 to 40%	80	6.0	25	34
41 to 50%	40	3.1	13	43
51 to 60%	20	1.7	32	55
Over 60%	0	0	n/a	n/a
All offenders	1,286	100	8.3	12

The majority (63%) of offenders granted HDC had a risk of reoffending within four months of below 10 per cent. The average risk of reoffending was 12 per cent, compared with 29 per cent for those not granted HDC. The actual percentage reconvicted was lower than predicted for those granted HDC, at just 8 per cent. This was driven by the low reoffending rates of those with predicted risks of over 20 per cent: while about 85 of these 254 were predicted to be reconvicted,[10] only 53 actually were. This finding, together with the low proportion of high-risk offenders granted HDC, suggests that when high-risk offenders did receive curfew it was often the result of a correct judgement about individual circumstances which made the offender a lower risk than the actuarial prediction alone suggested.

---

10 The average risk of reoffending within four months for this group was 33.6 per cent: 254*36 per cent=85.

Characteristics of those granted HDC

As Table 6.4 shows, the chance of being granted HDC was strongly, but not solely, dependent on offenders' predicted risk of reconviction. Table 6.5 shows that older offenders were, on average, more likely to be granted HDC.

Table 6.5: *Age of offender and assessment outcome*[11]

Age when eligible for HDC	Percentage of all programme group offenders	Percentage chance of being granted HDC
18-20	20.6	23
21-24	20.4	28
25-29	21.8	31
30-34	15.7	36
35-39	9.7	39
40-49	8.4	45
50 and over	3.6	44
All offenders	100	32

In showing that older offenders were more likely to be granted HDC, Table 6.5 accords with the findings reported in Chapter 3. However, it should be borne in mind that age is a significant predictor of detected reoffending, in that young offenders are, controlling for other factors, more likely to be reconvicted. The analysis therefore needs to be conducted in conjunction with the predicted rates of detected reoffending at four months. Table 6.6 displays the predicted and actual rates of reoffending of offenders of each age group granted and not granted HDC.

11 All percentages in Tables 6.5 and 6.7 have been weighted so that they reflect the actual percentage of offenders granted and not granted HDC, rather than the percentage among those studied. All percentages refer only to those who could be followed up for four months.

Table 6.6: **Predicted and actual rates of reoffending by age among offenders granted and not granted Home Detention Curfew**

Age when eligible for HDC	Granted HDC		Not granted HDC	
	Percentage predicted to reoffend within 4 months	Percentage reoffending within 4 months	Percentage predicted to reoffend within 4 months	Percentage reoffending within 4 months
18-20	17	17	37	45
21-24	16	13	33	33
25-29	13	8	30	29
30-34	11	5	25	28
35-39	9	5	21	23
40-49	6	1	15	12
50 and over	4	2	10	5
All offenders	12	8	29	31

Table 6.6 compares the predicted rates of reoffending with what actually occurred. It is clear that older offenders reoffended less than expected when granted HDC, even when controlling for predicted risk. The average predicted risk of those granted HDC was highest among younger offenders.

Analysis by gender shows no clear trend in the granting of HDC, with women comprising six per cent of both those granted and refused curfew. Detected reoffending rates are a few percentage points higher among women than men, whether or not curfew was granted, while there is little difference in predicted rates, but given the small number of women involved – just 75 were granted curfew – it is difficult to draw any conclusions from this.

Table 6.7 presents a breakdown of release rates by the type of criminal offence for which the offender was imprisoned.

Table 6.7: *Original criminal offence and assessment outcome*

Principal offence for which imprisoned	Percentage of all programme group offenders	Percentage chance of being granted HDC
Violence against the person	14.6	40
Sexual offence	2.3	4
Robbery	3.8	28
Burglary	16.7	22
Theft	18.7	22
Fraud	4.0	58
Drugs offence	8.7	59
Other offence	31.3	31
All offenders	100	32

Table 6.7 reveals that release rates were extremely low among sexual offenders.[12] Rates were also well below the average of 32 per cent when the original offence was burglary or theft. The highest release rates followed fraud and drugs convictions – at 59 and 58 per cent, these were about double the average for the other offence categories. Violent offenders were also curfewed at a higher than average rate.

Table 6.8 presents a similar analysis to Table 6.6, broken down by the principal offence for which the offender was imprisoned.

---

12 Very few sex offenders will have passed all the eligibility criteria. The recent Criminal Justice and Court Services Act (2000) has now made ineligible for HDC any offender required to register under the Sex Offenders Act (1997).

Table 6.8: **Predicted and actual rates of reoffending by original criminal offence among offenders granted and not granted Home Detention Curfew**

Principal offence for which imprisoned	Granted HDC		Not granted HDC	
	Percentage predicted to reoffend within 4 months	Percentage reoffending within 4 months	Percentage predicted to reoffend within 4 months	Percentage reoffending within 4 months
Violence against the person	8	6	20	20
Sexual offence	*	*	5	3
Robbery	14	2	27	21
Burglary	23	22	38	40
Theft	15	11	37	50
Fraud	6	2	12	15
Drugs offence	9	3	17	13
Other offence	12	8	28	27
All offenders	12	8	29	31

Note: Only 4 sexual offenders were granted curfew. The Criminal Justice and Court Services Act (2000) now rules out anyone required to register under the Sex Offenders Act (1997) from consideration for HDC.

Table 6.8 shows a comparison of actual and predicted reoffending for those granted and not granted HDC. Actual reoffending was lower than predicted among those convicted of robbery and drugs offences in particular. The very low level of reconviction of those originally convicted of robbery was, to an extent, reflected among those refused curfew. The overall pattern among curfewees of actual offending being several percentage points lower than predicted was broken by burglars, whose reoffending was almost exactly as predicted.

As with the analysis of age groups, it was apparent that the average risk of some groups of offenders not granted curfew (those convicted for sexual offences, fraud and, sometimes, drugs offences) was lower than that of some offenders granted curfew (those convicted of burglary, theft and robbery). The risk levels of sex offenders refused curfew are especially low, but it should be borne in mind that stringent conditions above and beyond an actuarial risk assessment needed to be satisfied for curfew to be granted to these offenders.[13] The low risk associated with non-curfewed fraud and drugs offenders suggests that some of these offenders will have not received curfew due to other factors such as accommodation, family consent, their behaviour in prison or the offenders' own wishes, rather than concerns that their criminal history made early reoffending likely.

---

13 As stated earlier, following the passing of the Criminal Justice and Court Services Bill, those required to register under the Sex Offenders Act (1997) are now excluded from consideration for HDC.

Conclusions

The level of reoffending, leading to reconviction, during the curfew period was just over 2 per cent. Offenders granted curfew had much lower reoffending rates after the end of the curfew than those refused, with eight per cent of curfewed offenders reoffending compared to 31 per cent of non-curfewed offenders. The overall reoffending rate of those eligible for curfew was very similar to that of a control group of offenders discharged before the scheme began and differences between the two groups were not statistically significant.

Release rates were much higher among offenders with low predicted risks of reoffending (obtained by adapting existing prediction tools based on previous and current offending and personal characteristics). When HDC was granted to offenders with high predicted risks, they offended less often than predicted, suggesting that release decisions in these cases effectively took account of individual circumstances.

While release rates were higher for older offenders, predicted and actual rates of reoffending amongst those granted curfew were highest for young offenders. Predicted and actual rates of reoffending were lowest among curfewees originally convicted of fraud and drugs offences and highest among curfewees originally convicted of theft and burglary. Risk also varied by age and criminal offence among those refused curfew.

Technical notes

Due to the short period of time available for follow-up of offenders and the importance of knowing the exact date of reoffending, the methodology of this study is innovative in some areas. This section expands on the explanation of this approach begun in the 'Methodology' section.

It should be clarified that the follow-up is based on date of reoffending rather than, as is customary in such studies, date of reconviction. The date of conviction is however used to control for the extra time available for control group reoffenders to be processed through the courts – for the purpose of this analysis, a reconviction is only counted if the conviction date is within six months of the offence date. For example, an offence committed on 5 August 1999 would only be counted as detected reoffending if the offender was convicted for the offence by 5 February 2000. Without this mechanism, control group members who were reconvicted, say, 18 months after reoffending would count as recidivists whereas programme group members who will find themselves in a similar situation, say at the beginning of 2001, would be counted as non-recidivists. The mechanism is therefore necessary to allow a like-for-like comparison between the control and programme groups.

The PNC data were extracted on 16 August 2000. After a follow-up period of a given number of months, plus a further six months for all admissible convictions to occur, a 'buffer' period of two months is allowed in order for police forces to enter data onto the PNC. (It is known that the police forces did not complete data entry by this point, but the declining numbers of offenders in the successive rows (months) of Table 6.2 should indicate that a lengthier buffer period would have made follow-up for more than one or two months impossible.) The follow-up period itself must therefore have been completed by 16 December 1999. This affects the number of offenders who can be followed-up for different periods of time, but is necessary in order to ensure consistent data quality. Offenders who cannot be tracked for the full eight months beyond the end of a follow-up period are excluded from the analysis of that follow-up period.

It should be noted that, due to under-recording of assessment results, information on offenders refused HDC was completed using centrally-held prison discharge records. A complete listing of all those eligible for HDC would have required reference to manual records at all establishments. The discharge data should correctly reflect when offenders were eligible for HDC in the vast majority of cases, though there may be inconsistencies due to additional days given for indiscipline during the final weeks of the custodial portion of the sentence. The prison discharge records were also used to generate the control group.

To ensure consistent data quality, the analysis only includes offenders for whom the PNC and prison records held a common sentence date for the term of imprisonment resulting in HDC, and the PNC record confirmed that the sentence was one of imprisonment. This assured that the correct offenders were being traced on the PNC and that the PNC record was not likely to contain errors of detail which could affect the counting of reconvictions. Offenders were also excluded if they received convictions which resulted in imprisonment for offences committed before the period of imprisonment for which they received HDC (these are known as *pseudoreconvictions*), as such imprisonments would prevent them being exposed to the risk of recidivism for the full length of the follow-up period.

It is possible to predict the risk of detected reoffending using existing actuarial[14] predictors of reconviction. The Prison Service uses its Sentence Planning Predictor during the risk assessment process. Analysis of the Police National Computer data showed that it is also possible to apply the Offender Group Reconviction Scale (OGRS) tool to this situation. While OGRS is designed for use with Offenders Index data on reconviction for a standard

---

14 'Actuarial' predictors rely solely on 'hard' data based on the conviction history and demographic characteristics of the offender. They are known to predict reoffending more accurately than judgement-based 'clinical' methods alone.

list offence within two years,[15] those with higher OGRS scores proved to have a higher probability of reoffending within the short follow-up periods available when evaluating HDC.

---

15 The Offenders Index is a database containing details of every conviction in England and Wales since 1963 for offences on the 'standard list'. The 'standard list' contains all indictable and a few summary criminal offences. While the Offenders Index is the standard source of reconviction data, it does not include the date of offence but only the date of conviction. It is therefore impossible to be sure whether an offence was actually committed within a particular short time period such as the duration of an HDC licence (as opposed to either just after the completion of the licence, or before the offender was initally imprisoned). To limit the effect of this shortcoming on the validity of an evaluation, follow-up periods of less than two years are discouraged. The Police National Computer does not have this limitation, but has only been available for evaluation work for a short time and no reconviction predictors have yet been designed especially for use with it.

7.   Conclusion

The Home Detention Curfew scheme running in England and Wales is one of the largest electronic monitoring programmes in the world. Together with the interim Research Findings (Dodgson and Mortimer, 2000), the findings of this report confirm that the scheme has been operating smoothly, with the assessment process focused clearly on risk.

The great majority of curfewees complete their HDC period successfully, with only five per cent being recalled to custody. However, there is some evidence that violations and recalls might be further reduced if prisoners were better prepared for, and supported after, release. The scheme has generated large cost savings over the first year of approximately £37 million and an analysis of reoffending by curfewees suggests that the effect of HDC is broadly neutral compared to a control group.

Releases and recalls

Approximately 4,500 prisoners per month have been eligible for Home Detention Curfew and following the risk assessment by staff in prison establishments and probation services, an average of 1,300 per month have been placed on HDC (a release rate of 30%) during the first 16 months of the scheme's operation. On average, there were almost 2,000 curfewees subject to HDC at any one time.

Variations in release rates appear to be closely linked to risk of reoffending and reimprisonment. Sub-groups of the prison population that are granted HDC less often than average tend to have higher than average risk scores and vice versa. There is no evidence from release rates that there is discrimination against women prisoners or prisoners from minority ethnic communities.

The rate of recall to prison following a breakdown in the curfew has remained low and steady over the first 16 months of the scheme, at around five per cent of curfewees. Over the period covered by this report, only eight curfewees (less than 1% of recalls) were returned to prison because they posed a risk of serious harm to the public. This suggests that prisons and probation services are carrying out the risk assessment thoroughly and conscientiously.

There is no clear link between release rates and recall rates – that is, those prisons that release a higher proportion of eligible inmates onto HDC are not associated with higher levels of recall following a breakdown of the curfew.

The impact of HDC on released prisoners

The generally successful operation of HDC was confirmed by the survey of curfewees, family members and supervising probation officers, suggesting that the scheme has had some degree of success in achieving its central aim of easing the transition from custody into the community. Respondents did, however, identify some areas where the scheme might be improved.

Curfewees were very positive about the scheme, with only two per cent saying that they would have preferred to spend the time in prison rather than on HDC. Other household members were also very positive about the scheme. Probation officers supervising those curfewees subject to non-HDC licences (in addition to the curfew) were also positive about the impact of HDC on their work with licencees.

There was some evidence that HDC is helping to influence prisoners' behaviour before release, including taking courses or jobs in the prison. There were, however, some concerns about the extent to which prisoners were prepared for the pressures they would face on HDC. Less than a third had seen the video in prison and one in six could not recollect being given anything in writing about the scheme's rules. Almost half felt that they were quite, or very poorly informed about the scheme prior to release and there is clearly scope for better briefing of both potential curfewees and others in the curfew household to help ensure the smoother running of the HDC period.

Over a third of curfewees interviewed had been able to find work while on HDC and a further third were seeking work. While the curfew provided advantages in helping released prisoners to develop a routine and look for work, it also posed difficulties for some who might not be able to find a job to fit with the curfew restrictions.

The contractor staff were praised by curfewees and household members as being polite, helpful and professional. Three-quarters of all respondents had been in contact with the probation service since release. Of these, two-thirds described their meetings as "generally helpful".

Just over three in five respondents said that they had experienced a curfew violation. However, nearly two-thirds of these claimed that the violation was down to equipment failure rather than any action (or inaction) on their own part. (These violations were as reported to interviewers by the curfewees; however, there does not appear to have been any widespread technical malfunctioning of electronic monitoring equipment over this period.)

A small sub-sample of recalled prisoners was also interviewed to discover the factors underlying their breaches of the curfew conditions. Some of the key issues here were: a lack of understanding of what the pressures of the curfew would be like; motivation and self-discipline of curfewees; support from family or friends; the impact of drug and alcohol use; housing problems; relationship problems; difficulties in keeping away from a life of crime; and lack of support to deal with problems.

There seems to be potential here for improving the scheme. Prisoners and their families need better information about HDC and how it will affect them. Ideally, prisoners should have access to this information before they apply and again before release to enable them to discuss any problems they might anticipate. There also needs to be clearer guidance for curfewees and families on what support is available for them after release.

Costs and benefits of HDC

Although the numbers released on HDC have not been as high as originally anticipated, the scheme has still generated considerable savings. The average period spent on curfew was 45 days, at a cost of approximately £1,300 per curfew (equivalent to £880 per month). The scheme has resulted in a net reduction in the prison population of 1,950 prison places during the first year of operation.

Taking into account the benefits of reducing pressure on the prison population, as well as the costs to prisons and probation services and the charges made by the electronic monitoring contractors, the Home Detention Curfew scheme has resulted in significant net benefits of £36.7 million over the first year of operation. The main driver for generating savings is the number of prisoners released on HDC.

Reoffending by curfewees

Taken as a whole and followed up over a six month post-release period, prisoners eligible for Home Detention Curfew offended at almost the same rate as a control group taken before the scheme was introduced. There were no statistically significant differences between the programme group and the control group. Within the group of eligible prisoners, there was a big difference between those granted HDC and those refused. In a six-month follow-up period from the automatic release date, those refused HDC were reconvicted for a new offence more than four times as often as those who were released on curfew. This provides further evidence of the thoroughness with which prison and probation staff carry out the risk assessment.

Implications

Home Detention Curfew has been relatively successful over the first 16 months of operation:

- there is evidence from the surveys of curfewees and supervising probation officers that the curfew can indeed help to provide a managed transition between custody and living in the community
- analysis of reoffending suggests that the impact of HDC is broadly neutral in terms of reconvictions for new offences
- HDC has generated large savings (£36.7 million in the first year alone) when compared with the cost of keeping the curfewees in prison.

As with any large-scale activity there are variations in the way it is operated and there are areas where the scheme could be made more efficient (some of which were the subject of a recent Practitioners Guide – see Dodgson, Mortimer and Sugg, 2000). However, such issues would probably be expected in a scheme of this scale and do not detract from the successful working of HDC. Overall, it has made a significant impact on prison life and has become a standard part of the work of prisons and probation services. The Home Detention Curfew scheme has established that a large-scale electronic monitoring programme involving several different agencies can be operated successfully and is consistent with an approach to release decisions which puts assessment of risk at the centre.

Dodgson, K. and Mortimer, E. (2000) *Home Detention Curfew – the first year of operation.* Research Findings No. 110. London: Home Office.

Dodgson, K., Mortimer, E. and Sugg, D. (2000) *Assessing prisoners for Home Detention Curfew: a guide for practitioners.* RDS Practitioners Guide No. 1. London: Home Office.

HM Prison Service. (2000) *Home Detention Curfew.* Prison Service Order No. 6700. London: HM Prison Service.

HM Prison Service. (2000) *Annual report and accounts: April 1999 to March 2000.* London: The Stationery Office.

Home Office. (2000) *Prison statistics England and Wales 1999.* London: The Stationery Office.

Home Office. (1999) *Home Detention Curfew information protocol.* London: Home Office.

Hood, R and Shute, S. (2000). *The parole system at work: a study of risk based decision-making.* Home Office Research Study No 202. London: Home Office.

Kershaw, C., Goodman, J. and White, S. (1999) *Reconvictions of offenders sentenced or discharged from prison in 1995, England and Wales.* Home Office Statistical Bulletin Issue No. 19/99. London: Government Statistical Service.

Mortimer, E. and May, C. (1997) *Electronic monitoring in practice: the second year of the trials of curfew orders.* Home Office Research Study No. 177. London: Home Office.

Notes

Notes

RDS Publications

Requests for Publications

Copies of our publications and a list of those currently available may be obtained from:

Home Office
Research, Development and Statistics Directorate
Communications & Development Unit
Room 201, Home Office
50 Queen Anne's Gate
London SW1H 9AT
Telephone: 020 7273 2084 (answerphone outside of office hours)
Facsimile: 020 7222 0211
E-mail: publications.rds@homeoffice.gsi.gov.uk

alternatively

why not visit the RDS web-site at
          Internet: http://www.homeoffice.gov.uk/rds/index.htm

where many of our publications are available to be read on screen or downloaded for printing.